Community Gardening

A PHS Handbook

Editor: Jane Carroll
Design: Eliza Whitney and Anne Vallery
Photographs: Margaret Funderburg and PHS staff, except where noted

Contributors
Jane Carroll
Janet Evans
Eileen Gallagher
Heidi Hiteshue
Julia Marano
Sally McCabe
Daniel Moise
Terry Mushovic
Jane G. Pepper
Pete Prown
Patricia Schrieber
Beverly Vandenburg

The Pennsylvania Horticultural Society
100 N. 20th St., 5th floor
Philadelphia, PA 19103

PHSonline.org

Drew Becher, President
Maitreyi Roy, Vice President for Programs
Patricia James, Director of Education
Pete Prown, Director of Publications

© 2010 Pennsylvania Horticultural Society
ISBN Number 978-0-615-40150-8
Record Number 52295

Acknowledgments

PHS wishes to thank the dedicated members of its community greening, education, and landscape design staff, both past and present, as well as the legions of community gardeners throughout Philadelphia and across the country.

Thanks also to the many partnering organizations that have worked with PHS to support, grow, and sustain community gardens.

Special thanks to the following supporters of PHS community gardening initiatives:

The Burpee Foundation
City of Philadelphia
Claneil Foundation
EP Henry
Greater Philadelphia Coalition Against Hunger
The Albert M. Greenfield Foundation
Gro 'n Sell
W.K. Kellogg Foundation/Gardenburger
Independence Foundation
KJK Associates
The Forrest C. & Frances H. Lattner Foundation
The Lenfest Foundation
Mennonite Foundation
Philadelphia Prison System
The Lawrence Saunders Fund
Snave Foundation
US Department of Agriculture, National Institute of Food and Agriculture
Ruth and A. Morris Williams, Jr.

Chapter 1: About Community Gardens

Introduction

This handbook reveals how people can work together to create thriving gardens that not only provide fresh food and fellowship, but also help build stronger, more livable neighborhoods. The book is intended as a resource for community gardeners throughout the country, who take patches of unused land and work together to transform them into green spaces that nourish, inspire, and unite communities.

A community garden is any garden tended collectively by a group of people. Community gardening has a long history in Europe and the United States. It has roots in the nineteenth century, when industrialization and overcrowding led to health concerns for city dwellers, especially children. Many schools at that time began gardening programs to give children access to fresh air and exercise. Europe has a strong tradition of "allotment gardens" on shared land with plots tended by generations of families.

Victory Gardens created during World Wars I and II fueled the community gardening movement. Many gardens were planted in shared public spaces, and the trend gained further momentum during the 1960s and 1970s as communities mobilized to address urban decay and environmental degradation. Many urban community gardens are built on unused vacant lots, while others are installed in parks or at faith-based institutions, community centers, and schools.

About the Pennsylvania Horticultural Society

The Pennsylvania Horticultural Society (PHS) is a nonprofit membership organization founded in 1827. PHS produces the **Philadelphia International Flower Show**®, the world's largest indoor flower show, and offers events, workshops, tours, and publications for gardeners at all levels of interest. Proceeds from the Flower Show, along with funding from foundations, corporations, government agencies, and individuals, help support PHS programs.

Education programs about gardening, horticulture, and improving public spaces are intrinsic to the PHS mission to *motivate people to improve the quality of life and create a sense of community through horticulture*. In addition to workshops for gardeners, the PHS Garden Tenders and Tree Tenders® training programs teach residents to create community gardens and plant and care for community trees. The Green City Teachers training program provides Philadelphia educators with the skills to integrate horticultural and environmental education into curricula, after-school programs, and service-learning projects. It also trains teachers to create and maintain school gardens. Programs for youth engage children in gardening and community stewardship.

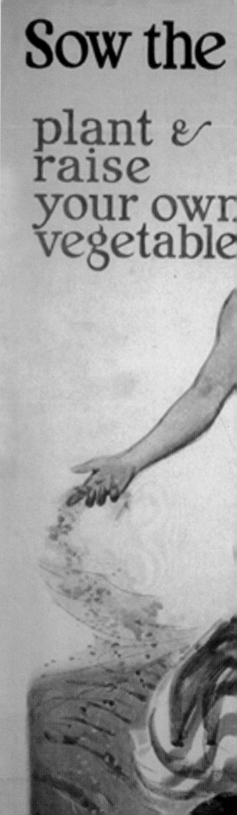

Sow the
plant &
raise
your own
vegetable

Posters like this one (circa 1918)
were meant to encourage the
planting of "war gardens."

Victory Gardens

During World War I and World War II, the concept of a "Victory Garden" in America grew in response to the need for more local food at a time when traditional food sources were diverted toward the war efforts. In Europe, this was also a pressing need since most of the farmers and food producers had gone off to war, leaving families to either keep farms going or start new vegetable gardens.

Inspired by slogans like "Will you have a part in victory?" and "Sow the seeds of Victory!", American citizens were exhorted to produce plants that would feed themselves and the local economy, as well as reduce pressure on the national food-production system. And it worked. During the latter days of World War I and throughout World War II, U.S. residents grew tons of vegetables and fruits, distributing them and canning them for future use. According to the National War Garden Commission, Americans created 2.2 million new garden plots in 1918 alone, and yielded more than 528.5 million pounds of produce (SOURCE: *sidewalksprouts.wordpress.com*).

More importantly, these Victory Gardens of the war years jump-started both the community gardening and urban-farming movements, both of which continue to thrive today. The act of learning how to garden and put fresh vegetables on the table empowered millions of people to take control of their own food supply.

Today, that lesson still reverberates. With food prices increasing and many people searching for an organic solution to feeding their families, the simple act of joining a community garden becomes a way for people to not only meet those needs, but also to bond with their neighbors. And that, surely, is a victory for everyone.

Eileen Gallagher

The Philadelphia Green Story

PHS's **Philadelphia Green**® program is the most comprehensive urban greening program in the nation. Through Philadelphia Green, PHS promotes investment in green infrastructure as a tool for community revitalization and economic development, contributing to Philadelphia's renaissance as a destination city.

Since 1974, Philadelphia Green has been working in partnership with government, community organizations, and residents to create, restore, enhance, and maintain community gardens, neighborhood parks, and civic landscapes and streetscapes in Philadelphia and beyond. It coordinates thousands of volunteers to plant and care for trees throughout the Greater Philadelphia Region and works with city government to transform blighted vacant lots into "clean and green" open spaces available for re-use.

Philadelphia Green also encourages citizens to become advocates for quality open space. It engages citizens in active dialog and public participation around the planning, design, and stewardship of new and restored green spaces.

Philadelphia Green's community gardening program began in the 1970s with two staff members and a truck. As the work grew throughout the 1980s and 1990s, Philadelphia Green supported fledgling community garden groups by providing soil, mulch, and fencing to establish new gardens. It also leveraged funding to offer ongoing material and technical support and established a network of Keystone Gardens—longstanding gardens that are recognized as important neighborhood institutions.

Responding to increased demand in the early 1990s, PHS launched the **Garden Tenders** training program to teach Philadelphians how to start and maintain community gardens on their own. The training has blossomed into a popular program that includes a range of practical information as well as hands-on horticulture (see page 10 for more on Garden Tenders).

In 2005 PHS created the **City Harvest** project, which supports a network of gardens that donate produce to area food cupboards. City Harvest is a partnership between PHS; the Philadelphia Prison System; SHARE (Self Help and Resource Exchange, a food distribution network); Weavers Way Co-op, and the Health Promotion Council of Southeastern Pennsylvania. The related City Harvest Growers Alliance promotes entrepreneurial urban food production. More information about City Harvest can be found on page 19.

How to Use this Handbook

Community Gardening: A PHS Handbook offers information and resources to help you develop the skills and knowledge to create and sustain a community garden. Topics range from organizing a garden group and securing land for gardening to formulating garden rules and dealing with challenges. Although the book draws on the experiences of PHS's Philadelphia Green program, it offers a framework of broad concepts and ideas that will be useful to gardeners in cities and towns across the nation.

The Resources section of the handbook shows you where to find additional information, including detailed gardening tips for your growing area. More information also can be found on the PHS website, *PHSonline.org,* or by contacting the PHS community greening staff at 215-988-8800.

PHS Garden Tenders

In 1995 PHS launched its **Garden Tenders training program** to teach Philadelphia residents how to create successful, self-sustaining community gardens.

Participants learn how to locate and secure permission to use a garden site, form a cohesive garden group, and plan and build their garden, as well as how to grow a host of plants, both edible and ornamental. They learn how to identify and tap into resources in the neighborhood, establish garden rules, deal with conflicts, raise funds for projects, and reach out to the community.

By the end of the training, Garden Tenders participants are expected to have formed a group, obtained permission to use their selected site, and completed a basic garden design. The final meeting is a workday at a garden site chosen by the class. But as Sally McCabe, who has been teaching Garden Tenders classes since the beginning, explains, "Often the groups are so enthusiastic they want to keep going week after week, long after the training formally ends." At the end of the course, a garden-building phase helps the groups get their ideas off the paper and into the ground.

Responsibility for upkeep of the gardens belongs to the garden group. Graduates of Garden Tenders create about 10 gardens per year in Philadelphia, and PHS offers workshops for continued learning.

The Garden Tenders model has led to the creation of a related PHS training program, **Green City Teachers**, which trains Philadelphia schoolteachers how to integrate horticulture into their curricula; it also guides teachers through the steps of creating and installing a school garden. For more information on these programs, please visit *PHSonline.org*.

"Often the garden groups are so enthusiastic
they want to keep going week after week,
long after the training formally ends."
— Sally McCabe of PHS

Community gardens, such as The Spring Gardens (at left), in Philadelphia, contribute to the economic health of neighborhoods.

The Value of Community Gardens

Community gardens offer important environmental, social, aesthetic, and economic benefits, not only for the people who tend them, but also for their wider surroundings. The **aesthetic benefits** of gardens are obvious. Community gardeners create a positive use for urban land that may have been blighted or neglected. Gardens add beauty and vibrancy to the landscape, especially in densely built cities. In addition, research shows that community gardens give cities an **economic** boost by increasing nearby property values and contributing to a high quality of life that attracts and retains residents.

Community gardens provide important **social benefits** as well. They strengthen community ties by creating a shared space for neighbors and forging bonds between residents, often bridging intergenerational and cross-cultural divides. Gardens can reflect and celebrate the cultural or ethnic traditions of neighborhoods. Community gardens help reduce crime by occupying spaces that may otherwise serve as havens for criminals and by bringing people outside as the eyes and ears of the neighborhood. Once neighbors realize the power and impact of gardening together, they are often inspired to collectively tackle other projects or to address other community needs.

Community gardens provide an ideal opportunity for engaging young people, senior citizens, and those in healthcare settings. Gardens offer a wealth of learning opportunities for children, and many garden groups reach out to local schools and after-school clubs. The healing aspects of gardens make them ideal for senior citizens, hospitals, and rehabilitation centers.

The most tangible benefit of community gardening is the **food** itself. Community gardeners benefit from fresh food and from the substantially lower cost of home-grown food over store-bought produce. Food gardening becomes more prevalent during times of economic hardship, and with heightened concern about food safety, healthy eating, and childhood obesity, there is a growing interest in edible gardening.

Lisa Taranto

The Tricycle Community Garden in Richmond, Virginia, began as a single community garden (the city's first) on a vacant lot owned by the Better Housing Coalition. The site has since grown to encompass four community gardens, three learning gardens, a greenhouse, and an urban farm.

Community gardens engage children
in the natural world.

In many inner-city neighborhoods, community gardens have long provided an
important source of fresh produce where it may otherwise be difficult to obtain.
Community gardeners have always had informal ways of sharing surplus vegetables
with neighbors and friends. Many cities and garden networks are helping to address
food scarcity by setting up formal systems to share garden bounty with less-fortu-
nate citizens.

Community gardens provide **environmental benefits** and can serve as models
for stewardship of natural areas. Simply by preserving open green space, gardens
improve air quality and absorb rainwater, reducing flooding and filtering pollution
from storm runoff. They provide nourishment and shelter for birds and beneficial
insects. Many community gardeners practice organic growing methods, use solar
panels for electricity, install rain barrels to conserve water, and turn garden waste
into compost. Because it requires less energy for transportation, locally grown food
helps reduce greenhouse-gas emissions. And many community gardens are grown
on vacant land that might otherwise attract trash and illegal dumping.

Community gardens provide inspiration for the growing trend toward **urban agriculture and locally produced food**. Urban agriculture not only serves as a use for
unused urban land, but also offers the promise of a new source of revenue and jobs.

quick tip

Once neighbors realize the power and
impact of gardening together, they are
often inspired to collectively tackle other
projects or to address other community
needs.

Sustainable Cities

Recognizing the benefits of community gardens, many municipalities invest resources to support and promote them. Some cities supply mulch, compost, and tools and make water accessible and affordable.

Two notable examples are Chicago and Seattle. Chicago helps negotiate leases for gardeners, leverages private funding, and makes park land available for garden plots. Seattle's extensive P-Patch program maintains several gardens in a land trust; employs paid staff; helps secure land leases for new gardens; and provides water, materials, training, and organizational support. Companion projects involve youth in gardens at public housing sites and help promote urban farming enterprises in low-income communities.

In other cities, nonprofit organizations help promote and support community gardens. In Philadelphia, the Pennsylvania Horticultural Society has a long history of helping community gardens with materials, technical assistance, and training. The Neighborhood Gardens Association/A Philadelphia Land Trust works to ensure preservation of community-managed gardens and helps gardeners secure long-term leases or permanent use of gardening sites. The Pennsylvania State University Cooperative Extension offers free gardening information and workshops.

Providing a good quality of life is a priority for twenty-first-century American cities competing for jobs and residents, and "greener" cities come out ahead. Many local governments are adopting sustainable practices, embracing green technologies, and encouraging environmental stewardship. Long a mainstay of the urban greening movement, community gardens will continue to play a vital role.

Lynne De Merritt

Seattle's P-Patch: A Model of Municipal Support

Through its extensive P-Patch program, the city of Seattle has made a long-term commitment to supporting and expanding community gardens. P-Patch employs paid staff; helps secure land leases for new gardens; and provides water, materials, training, and organizational support. A partner organization called the P-Patch Trust provides insurance and financial services, acquires land for permanent garden use, and promotes food-security programs. Funded by Seattle's Department of Neighborhoods, the P-Patch network encompasses more than 70 gardens.

One of the largest P-Patch gardens is the Magnuson Community Garden (left), a four-acre garden located within the 350-acre Warren G. Magnuson Park, Seattle's second-largest park. Among the garden's many standout features is a terraced amphitheater adorned with a graceful arbor that provides shade. Designed by Barker Landscape Architects with community input, the garden includes 140 individual plots, ponds, a children's garden, and a native plant border.

The PHS City Harvest project makes fresh food grown in community gardens available to food cupboards.

The City Harvest Story

In too many inner-city neighborhoods, it's easier to find a fast-food restaurant than a supermarket. As a consequence, some families experience hunger or eat unhealthful foods simply because their choices, or their means, are limited. According to the Food Resource Action Center (*www.frac.org*), 40.8 million Americans participated in the U.S. government's Supplemental Nutrition Assistance Program (food stamps) in May 2010, a record level. In Philadelphia, PHS helps address food hardship by tapping the skills and energy of community gardeners to make fresh produce more readily available.

Launched in 2006 with a founding grant from the Albert M. Greenfield Foundation, the PHS City Harvest program is a partnership between PHS; the Philadelphia Prison System; SHARE (Self Help and Resource Exchange, a food distribution network); Weavers Way Co-op; and the Health Promotion Council of Southeastern Pennsylvania.

Inmates of the Philadelphia Prison System start seeds at a prison greenhouse, receiving life-skills lessons in the process. Thousands more seeds are started in a greenhouse at Weavers Way Farm in northwest Philadelphia. The seedlings are transplanted into more than 40 participating community gardens throughout the city, as well as in the prison's Roots-to-Reentry garden. Participating gardens receive materials and training from PHS.

Prison inmates and volunteer gardeners grow the plants to maturity and, with help from SHARE, the resulting produce is distributed to food cupboards, where clients can take part in tastings, nutrition workshops, and cooking demonstrations offered by the Health Promotion Council. City Harvest gardeners donate an average of 13,000 pounds of produce each year.

With a grant from the U.S. Department of Agriculture in 2009, PHS added an entrepreneurial component aimed at further expanding the availability of locally grown fruits and vegetables. The **City Harvest Growers Alliance** is a network of independent growers who grow and sell produce for supplemental income. In exchange for materials such as seeds, plants, and lumber for raised beds, participants must attend workshops on sustainable food production and marketing, volunteer some of their time to the program, and donate a portion of their produce to City Harvest.

The City Harvest Growers Alliance supports a goal of Philadelphia's sustainability plan, *Greenworks Philadelphia*. It calls for establishing more food-producing gardens, urban farms, and farmers markets to bring fresh food to within 10 minutes of 75 percent of city residents by 2015.

Types of Community Gardens

Community gardens are as varied as the communities that give rise to them, reflecting the aspirations, purposes, and interests of the people who create and tend them. The following are examples of types of community gardens:

Food Gardens

The neighborhood food garden is the most common type of community garden in the United States. Usually located in urban settings, these gardens feature individual or household plots within a larger garden, typically surrounded by fencing. Most neighborhood community gardens have a defined leadership or committee structure, charge membership dues, and set garden guidelines that address upkeep and care of common spaces.

Flower Gardens or Combination Gardens

Gardeners may decide to create an ornamental garden for the exclusive use of the gardeners; for the enjoyment of the wider neighborhood; or for a faith community, hospital, library, or in parks or other public spaces. Many food gardeners incorporate ornamental gardening by adding plants with visual appeal to the garden entrance or in sitting areas.

Entrepreneurial Community Gardens

Some community gardens include a small business venture or job-training program. These gardens are frequently associated with youth programs but can serve other populations such as incarcerated individuals or those involved in substance-abuse recovery. Participants can gain valuable skills such as marketing, team-building, and job-readiness in addition to learning about horticulture. By selling the garden's produce, they can also earn money for their program.

Gardening to Fight Hunger

Some community gardeners may donate some or all of their produce to needy residents of their communities. They may partner with a local institution or participate in a larger initiative, such as the national "Share the Harvest" network or "Plant a Row for the Hungry" program.

Habitat Gardens

Gardeners sometimes work together to create an entire garden or a section of a garden specifically for wildlife, especially birds and beneficial insects. These gardens usually focus on native plants that provide food, shelter, and water for wild creatures. Habitat gardens make an excellent choice for schools, since students can study natural processes and the interaction between plants and animals. The National Wildlife Federation has a certification program for habitat gardens.(*http://nwf.org/backyard*)

School Gardens

School gardens help teachers integrate learning about the natural world into their curricula, serving as outdoor classrooms where children can study life sciences, math, art, social studies, and more. School gardens are usually created and managed by a teacher or group of teachers working with students, sometimes with the involvement of parents or neighborhood organizations. After-school programs and youth clubs such as Boy Scouts and Girl Scouts or 4-H clubs also make use of school gardens.

Rain Gardens

Sited in low-lying or moist areas, rain gardens are increasingly being used in built environments to help divert and absorb storm runoff. Rain gardens allow water to absorb into the ground and filter impurities from it, reducing pollution of rivers and streams. Rain gardens often focus on native species and feature plants that tolerate wet soils, such as wetland plants, rushes, sedges, and certain shrubs and trees.

Therapeutic or Healing Gardens

Hospitals, nursing homes, rehabilitation facilities, and substance-abuse programs are ideal settings for healing gardens, which are often built to accommodate people with disabilities. These gardens provide respite for clients and their families and caregivers, encourage active engagement of clients, and promote mental and physical wellbeing. Trickling water, shade-giving trees, and aromatic or medicinal herbs are common features of healing gardens.

Edible Landscapes

While many community food gardens devote space to ornamental gardening, a recent trend promotes mixing edible and ornamental plants in the same bed or growing area. Edible gardening focuses on food-producing plants, such as fruit and nut trees, berry bushes, herbs, and vegetables, arranged in aesthetically pleasing designs and/or planted in combination with strictly ornamental plants. For more on edible landscapes, please see page 80.

Julie Snell

The Gardens of Norris Square: Celebrating Culture

In some ethnically distinct neighborhoods, community gardens promote and strengthen a shared cultural identity. In Norris Square, a predominately Puerto Rican community in Philadelphia, six prize-winning gardens reflect pride in the rich heritage of area residents.

Las Parcelas is the largest of the gardens maintained by the Norris Square Neighborhood Project with support from PHS's Philadelphia Green program. Gardeners in 20 plots grow a wide variety of crops, including food found in Puerto Rican cuisine. The garden includes "La Casita," a small house that serves as a hub for celebrations and gatherings and features cooking utensils, home-made crafts, and musical instruments. Other gardens recognize the lesser-known African and Taino (the indigenous people of the island) aspects of Puerto Rican ancestry. The Norris Square community gardens serve as a meeting place for children's programs; as a hub for a local women's empowerment group, Grupo Motivos; and as a location for festivals and events.

"We want our youth to be proud of who they are and where they come from," says community leader Iris Brown. "Our gardens are special because we mix horticulture with culture."

Eileen Gallagher

Chapter 2: Organizing a Community Garden Group

Gauging Interest & Getting Started

Starting a community garden requires two obvious things: community and a garden. To start a garden group, all you need is people. Generate interest by asking friends and neighbors. The size of the group is flexible. In this early phase, don't feel as though you need to recruit enough people to fill every imagined plot. For now just gauge the level of interest in the community and join forces with others who are enthusiastic about a garden.

Once you have established a core group of at least three to five people, it's time to organize the first meeting. Use this meeting as an opportunity to bounce ideas off one another and come up with a vision for the garden. Remember that even though you as an individual may have come up with the idea, you cannot do it alone, or it won't be a community garden. Think in terms of the little "I" and the big "WE."

At the first meeting you should discuss:

- Who is available and interested in participating.
- What sort of garden this will be. Discuss the possibilities and develop an overall vision.
- Where you want the garden to be. Does the group have a site in mind?
- When you think this can become a reality. Set up a timeline with specific goals.
- Why the group wants this garden. Draft a mission statement that spells out the guiding principles and ideals for the garden.

Once the group has answered the five Ws, it's time for the obvious H: How. Ideas are great, but an action plan is a must. Determine how the group will proceed from here and be prepared to meet regularly to monitor progress. This planning period lays important groundwork for everything to come.

Finding Fellow Gardeners

Once the core group is established, reach out to the community. You can circulate a simple petition, questionnaire, or email asking people for their support of the garden project and whether or not they may be interested in a plot (see sample questionnaire on page 55).

Another option is to hold a neighborhood meeting. Spread the word about the meeting on flyers (with all the essential information) distributed around town at schools, libraries, places of worship, and businesses. Other avenues for communicating your message include the local newspaper, your Facebook page or other social media. Have a sign-in sheet at the meeting to gather names and contact information.

Using the meeting management suggestions on page 38, take this opportunity to get a dialog going. Have an open and inclusive process and be responsive to people's input and concerns. Find out what they want for and from a garden.

Before the meeting concludes, be sure to have some concrete next steps to get the community garden off the ground. Once you have a list of interested gardeners, create a method for keeping them informed of upcoming events and other items. Decide as a group whether this means weekly emails, a phone tree, or regular meetings. Be sure to share responsibilities.

Promoting Diversity

One of the most rewarding aspects of community gardening is the way it can bring together people from different walks of life, so encourage diversity among the garden group. Bringing together people of varied backgrounds and life experiences will enrich your garden group. Someone from a different culture could introduce you to your new favorite vegetable. Perhaps a transplant from a rural area has farming skills to share. There's so much a group of gardeners stand to learn from one another, and the friendships formed will be as cherished as the time you spend tending your plot.

Providing Your Garden Group with Structure & Leadership

Each person involved in the community garden is likely to feel passionately about his or her specific plot, but who will look out for the garden as a whole? Your group will need to establish some sort of governing body to help steer the overall vision and tackle the "big picture" matters.

There is no one-size-fits-all leadership structure. Some gardens opt to elect a president who has the final word in decision making. This person may hold the position for a set period of time. Other gardens prefer a steering committee or leadership council.

Large garden groups may need committees focused on specific aspects of the garden, such as membership, watering, and mulching. Depending on your leadership structure, perhaps the committee heads can collectively form the community garden's leadership council, or they can serve as the garden president's "cabinet."

Although leadership is essential, a community garden president may soon feel overworked if he or she shoulders too much responsibility alone. Delegating not only spreads the workload, but also helps prepare the next leader. Also, no one likes a dictator, so all participants should have a voice when it comes to the garden. Be sure that everyone has an outlet for sharing ideas, concerns, and news. Tap everyone for planning and problem solving.

Eileen Gallagher

29

Establishing a Charter and Guidelines

To solidify your community garden group as something real and lasting, get things down on paper or a laptop. First up is a charter, which provides the framework for productive collaboration. Once the core group is established, devote a meeting to drafting this document.

The charter should give a brief synopsis of the garden and address its purpose. If your group wants to compose a mission statement, this is the place for it. It could be something along the lines of …

The Main Street Community Garden is a welcoming space for Springfield residents to raise vegetables and flowers, promote unity and friendship, and beautify the neighborhood. As gardeners we strive to make the Main Street Community Garden a haven of respect, awareness, and community.

The charter should also detail the procedural operations of the garden. This includes protocol on how plots are assigned, how new members are selected, how decisions are made, and how leadership is appointed. This document doesn't require elaborate language; just make it clear and communicative. At this stage, don't belabor every point; draft a good basic charter and vote on it.

Next you'll need to spell out the garden guidelines or rules. These can either be folded into your charter or serve as a separate document, but whereas the charter captures the "big picture" ideas, the rules address the day-to-day operations of the garden.

Garden guidelines should cover the following topics:

- Establishment of plot fees and expectations on the number of meetings gardeners must attend.

- Housekeeping practices regarding upkeep of plots, common spaces, pathways, compost piles, and any permanent fixtures.

- Matters of courtesy such as where people should park their cars, whether pets are allowed in the garden, trash collection, and the policy for borrowing communal tools and supplies.

- Security issues like who locks the garden gate at night, how vandalism is addressed, and the age at which children are allowed to be in the garden unsupervised.

- A "Hold Harmless," or indemnity, clause. This is very important. Make sure all community gardeners understand that the landowner or the garden group cannot be held responsible if a gardener is injured while he or she is in the garden. Gardeners must acknowledge that they are willingly participating in this activity and that, like anything in life, there are certain risks. The distribution of Hold Harmless forms is also an opportunity to review safety and security practices for your garden.

These documents will prove their worth when the garden group experiences challenges. For example, some gardeners will be vigilant caretakers of their plots, while others may view the garden as more of a hobby to attend to when time allows. This disparity can be difficult to manage; the key is to be respectful of everyone and have the rules serve as the final word. To minimize conflicts, have all present and future gardeners (and the landowner, if applicable) sign off on the charter and/or rules.

Although it's an unpleasant topic, the garden guidelines should be explicit about the process of expulsion. Clearly state the grounds and the process for expulsion (usually after a few warnings).

Revisit your charter and garden rules yearly as a group, amending them when necessary. What is important today might not be relevant a year from now, so the garden rules must adapt to the changing needs and concerns of the gardeners.

Southwark/Queen Village Community Garden: Fine-Tuning Garden Management

South Philadelphia's Southwark/Queen Village Community Garden is a welcome oasis of beauty and open space in a densely built neighborhood. Arguably the most impressive aspect of the Southwark garden is its longevity. In operation for more than 30 years, it is easily one of the longest-standing community gardens in Philadelphia. The garden site is now held by the Neighborhood Gardens Association/A Philadelphia Land Trust. (See page 57 for more on land trusts.)

Southwark gardener Ed Mitinger credits the garden's durability to a core group of members and leaders working toward a shared goal. This group—which includes some of the garden's founders—strives for the betterment of the community as a whole, and encourages gardeners to think of themselves as a unit, as opposed to individuals occupying the same space.

Over the past three decades the Southwark gardeners have developed a highly organized management structure that includes committees and a rotating leadership system. The president and other leaders serve terms of two years, and all members vote on important issues so that everyone has a say.

While this system succeeds at Southwark, Ed stresses that each community garden functions differently, and that the leadership must "reflect the people who started it and those who grow there now. Any would-be garden leader should find a style that works for his or her particular garden and find a common objective to unite participants and keep them coming back."

At Southwark, all gardeners are held to a high standard regarding maintenance of plots, and a comprehensive list of rules and expectations is understood and enforced. Gardeners are also expected to attend meetings and garden cleanups.

Because of this organized system, the Southwark garden has become a vibrant hub of the neighborhood. The garden has participated in the PHS City Harvest program for five years, donating thousands of pounds of fresh produce to a food bank across the street, which mostly serves senior citizens.

With a commendable 30-year legacy, one can easily imagine the Southwark/Queen Village Garden going strong for many more decades.

Community Garden Rules

- The basic fee for a garden plot is $10 annually, payable no later than May 30 of each year.

- Garden meetings are held the second Thursday of each month during the gardening season: April through September.

- Individual plots must be cleared and started no later than May 1 or they will be given to the next person on the waiting list and the plot fee returned to the original applicant.

- Each gardener is responsible for weeding and clearing his/her plot, the paths around it, the adjacent fence line, and the outside of the fence.

- Each gardener is expected to spend at least four hours per week working on his/her plot and the surrounding areas.

- Gardening activity and plant growth must be restricted to the gardener's plot. Please prevent vegetation from interfering with walkways and adjacent plots.

- Each gardener is responsible for trash removal.

- Garden plots in weedy and neglected condition by July 4 will be cleared. They will be given to existing gardeners for fall planting only and will be open for new gardeners the following season.

- Pesticide and chemical fertilizer use by gardeners is prohibited. Violators will lose their plots, and their plot fees will be returned.

- Stay out of other people's plots unless specifically invited.

- Pets brought into the garden should be restrained on a leash, and the person responsible must clean up any droppings, food, etc.

- If for any reason (health, vacation, work demands) you will be temporarily unable to maintain your plot, inform the coordinator. If you have a substitute gardener, inform the coordinator.

- ALL gardeners will participate in group garden activities such as mulching pathways, general cleanup, and preparation for special events.

- At the end of the season, all dead plants and weeds not suitable for composting should be removed, bagged, and placed at curbside on trash day.

- Non-compliance with these rules will lead to two warnings and then to expulsion. You will lose your plot, and your plot fee will be returned.

- Any rules to be added or eliminated later must be passed by the majority of the participating gardeners.

- **I understand that neither the garden group nor owners of the land are responsible for my actions. I therefore agree to hold harmless the garden group and owners of the land for any liability, damage, loss, or claim that occurs in connection with use of the garden by me or any of my guests.**

I understand all these rules and regulations and promise to follow them in good conscience.

Print Name _____

Address _____

Phone _____

Email _____

Signature _____

Date _____

Please sign and return one copy. Keep another copy for reference.

Insurance Matters

In your community garden charter, guidelines, or perhaps a separate document, make it clear that neither the garden nor the landowner is to be held liable for injuries or damage to property that may occur at the site. Having the gardeners sign off on this makes them aware of the risks of participation from the start. This precaution, however, may prove insufficient if a lawsuit arises. Therefore, consider obtaining insurance. (Some landowners may require you to do so.)

There is no one-size-fits-all insurance policy when it comes to community gardens, and many insurance agents have difficulty determining how to classify them. Land ownership is sure to be one of the central factors when it comes to devising an insurance policy. Your group's status as a 501(c)(3) or the possibility of it being absorbed by an existing nonprofit or land trust are also relevant considerations.

The first step in pursuing insurance is consulting an insurance agent or attorney. Ask your fellow gardeners if they have a friend, relative, or acquaintance who works in the industry and see if he or she will be willing to offer guidance.

Store a copy of the insurance policy and other important documents in a safe place. This aspect of forming a garden may seem overwhelming, but don't let it deter you from your ultimate goal of creating a great neighborhood space.

Determining Membership Dues

The majority of community gardens charge members seasonal or annual plot fees or dues. This fee helps offset the basic costs of running and maintaining the garden and can help build a nest egg that can be tapped in lean times or when unexpected costs arise.

How much does a garden plot cost? When trying to pinpoint a dollar amount to charge the gardeners, first get a feel for your expenses. But at the same time, keep fees nominal and make sure they are affordable for members of your community. Basic garden expenses often include:

- Rent paid to the landowner (if applicable)
- Utilities (water, electricity, etc.)
- Purchasing and maintaining tools
- Bulk purchases of soil or mulch
- Insurance

Once you have a good sense of basic expenses, it will be easier to determine the dollar amount of dues. Also take a look at other possible sources of revenue. You may decide to hold fundraising events, form partnerships, or seek out grants. (See page 45 for more on fundraising.)

Remember that fees serve a purpose beyond recouping costs. When people have put their hard-earned money into the garden—even a few dollars—they literally become invested in its future.

Creating a Wait List

Perhaps the best problem your garden can face is having too many eager participants and not enough plots. If this happens, start a waiting list. Develop a form for these individuals to fill out and keep all requests on file. For the sake of fairness, the earliest respondent should be the first contacted if a plot becomes available.

Before a new gardener joins the fold, give him or her a copy of the charter and rules. Ask the applicant to read them thoroughly and request a signature when the person joins so there is no misunderstanding as to the commitment being made.

Developing Goals

Goals keep people focused and productive. Much like running a business, it is beneficial to set both short-term and long-term goals and have them guide your efforts. Common goals might include acquiring a certain number of new gardeners, raising funds for a project, or planning and hosting events.

Of course you can't set goals without also establishing a budget. Assess all costs and revenue and reach a firm understanding of your financial picture. With that information in hand you'll be able to develop goals that are strategic and realistic.

When goals are met, celebrate! Recognition and encouragement will make people more likely to take on additional projects in the future.

Garden Meetings

Meetings provide the opportunity to get organized, share information and ideas, solve problems, and celebrate your garden group's accomplishments. Regularly scheduled meetings keep the lines of communication open and help keep the group on task. But never have a meeting just to meet; if there is nothing to discuss, cancel the meeting. Respect people's time and strive to conduct meetings that are focused and productive. Make the schedule easy to remember (e.g., the third Monday of the month at 7 pm).

When organizing a meeting, ask yourself:
- What is the purpose of the meeting?
- What will people know, feel, and do as a result of attending the meeting?

Other meeting tips include:

Assign Roles
Decide who will manage or facilitate the meeting and who will introduce which topics. Ask for volunteers to take notes and keep track of time.

Set an Agenda
Draw up an agenda. Decide ahead of time what will be discussed and how much time you will spend. Allow time at the end of the meeting for review.

Establish Decision-Making Policies
Decision-making is where many groups falter. Be sure participants understand their role in the process. Decide what constitutes a quorum—the minimum number of people who must be present to make an important group decision. Be clear about how a decision will be made prior to calling for a vote.

What if the group is not ready to make a decision? Determine what people need in order to take a position. Do they simply need more time to consider the issues? Do they need more information? Based on these needs, identify the next steps with a division of labor and time frame.

Delegate
Conclude each meeting with a good sense of the "next steps." List upcoming initiatives and clarify tasks, division of labor, and time frame necessary to keep the work moving forward.

Dealing with Conflict

Conflicts are inevitable and present a challenge for many groups. If handled poorly, conflicts can tear a group apart, so the tendency is to avoid them. Resolving conflicts in a constructive way requires skill, patience, and courage, but it will make the group stronger in the long run. The following tips will help you navigate conflicts, but they are useful for any meeting facilitator:

Actively Listen

Listen carefully with an open mind and heart to what people are saying. Don't finish other people's sentences or prepare a defense while someone else is speaking. True listening is more than waiting for your turn to talk.

Paraphrase

Repeat what you are hearing, without judgment, and check for accuracy: "So what I'm hearing is … Is that what you mean?"

Summarize

Summarize the different points of view.

Analyze

Have the group think about the pros and cons of each position.

Resolve or Advance

Find out if the group is ready to make a decision or come to an agreement about how to proceed. If not, ask what people need to move forward, such as more time to think, more time to discuss the issue, or a third party to help mediate.

Communication: Getting Your Garden Group Online

Thanks to technology, it's easier than ever to communicate with your fellow gardeners. Here are a few ways to maximize the Web's potential:

Facebook

Facebook has become a popular form of web-based communication. If most of the gardeners have Facebook accounts, set up a page that will allow them to share ideas, upload photo albums, and post links to other relevant sites. You can also use Facebook's Wall and News Feed functions to keep everyone informed.
      WEB SOURCES: *Facebook.com*

Email

Email is a simple way to quickly share information. Create a group (or distribution list) in your email program. Most programs allow the user to create a group by add-

How to Reach a Group Decision

- **Consensus**: An opinion or position agreed to by the group as a whole.
- **Simple Majority:** A number of voters constituting more than half the total.
- **Two-thirds Majority:** The number of votes for a proposition equalling or exceeding twice the number of votes against it.
- **Plurality:** The largest voting bloc, even if it falls short of a majority of the group.
- **Range Voting:** Each participant ranks or scores the available options using a point system.

ing a number of email addresses and then saving them under one name (such as "The 2nd Street Gardeners"). Then, whenever you type "The 2nd Street Gardeners" into the address line, everyone on your distribution list will receive that email.

Blogging

A blog is another great option. A blog is essentially a webpage that allows designated people to post messages and photos. Use the blog to tell gardeners about upcoming dates or to share information. Best of all, most blog pages are free. The only downside of blogs for a group is that it's basically a one-way form of communication—from the writer to the reader.

SOURCES: *Blogspot.com* and *Wordpress.com*

Groups

Another choice for communication is a web forum. For example, a Yahoo or Google Group is a web-oriented group formed around a single subject. After it's launched, the group moderator can decide who may join, which can be anyone surfing the web or just those who are part of the garden. All members of your group can write messages and respond to messages by others. Like many blog sites, groups are free of charge.

SOURCES: *Yahoogroups.com* and *Groups.Google.com*

Web Calendars

This is a service (often free) that allows groups to share an online calendar. Members of these groups can post events and receive reminders of upcoming events.

SOURCES: *Google.com/calendar* and *Calendar.Yahoo.com*

Website

With sufficient time and resources, a garden group may choose to create its own website. A website can be very simple—just a few pages with basic information, important dates, and a photo or two.

Self-Built Sites

Most Internet providers give their members free software to create a website, as well as a small amount of server space to host a website for free (websites require physical hard-drive space to exist). Check with your provider for more information on these self-built and often free sites.

SOURCES: *iGoogle.com, AOL.com, Earthlink.net,* and *Joomla.org*

Using a Web Developer … or a Friend!

You may decide to hire a web developer to build a site for the garden. The developer will meet with you to discuss the site's functions and then help design the required pages. Be sure to agree on a price for services and a timetable for completion. You should also talk about long-term hosting of the site, as well as who will handle updates.

Sometimes the easiest and most affordable way to build a website is to ask a tech-savvy gardener or friend to build your site for free or at a discount. Just be clear on roles and expectations; talk about what you want from the site and when you need it completed. And, as with all volunteers, remember to say, "Thank you!"

SOURCES: *Web-development.com* and *Freelancedesigners.com*

While the Internet is a tremendous resource, remember that some people involved with the garden may not use computers regularly. This is especially true among older people and in low-income neighborhoods. Ensure that these people are not excluded from discussions and that there are alternative means of sharing information.

Creating a Safe Space

In many cities, crime, especially vandalism, is one of the risks of community gardening. To keep the garden and its gardeners safe, encourage members to visit the garden in pairs and set gardening hours, such as sun-up to sundown. A fence with a lockable gate is an obvious way to keep out unwanted visitors. You may also consider a sign that lets people know the garden is carefully watched, such as "This garden is maintained by neighbors. Visiting hours are 4 to 8 pm."

Another way to keep the garden safe is ensuring that all the gardeners get to know each other well; that way outsiders are easily identified. Bring gardeners together frequently for meetings and celebrations so they can form a strong, united team.

Even if they aren't gardeners, the people who live adjacent to the garden are still invested in keeping their block and community safe. Communicate with them your shared interests and ask them to help serve as your eyes and ears. As a thank you, share some of your harvest.

In the event of vandalism, repair damage immediately. By quickly removing all signs of vandalism, it sends a message to the culprits that their behavior won't be tolerated. Show them that you will not be disheartened or deterred, and eventually they will lose interest.

By all means, reach out to the local police force and ask them to keep an eye out for the garden, especially late at night. If a problem arises, let them handle the situation.

Funding and Sustaining Your Community Garden

There are no two ways about it, launching and maintaining a community garden costs money. And while membership dues can cover basic expenses, your group may need to raise funds for more ambitious projects like building a tool shed, purchasing supplies, or installing solar panels. The group may also need to occasionally pay for services such as concrete work, signage, or fencing.

Fundraising is far simpler when a group is organized. Your group will need to agree on priorities and develop a clear, well-thought-out strategy.

One way to raise money is by organizing a special event. This can be as simple as a bake sale, flea market, raffle, car wash, silent auction, or concert. Fund-raising events are also good opportunities for recruiting new gardeners.

A second approach is to target certain sectors of your community. Consider approaching the following groups for assistance:

Community institutions
Start with organizations in your neighborhood such as religious institutions, colleges, parent-teacher organizations, and community groups (Kiwanis, garden clubs, etc.).

Local businesses
Ask home and garden centers, hardware stores, print shops, supermarkets, and coffee shops for donations or in-kind services. Sometimes receiving supplies or products (or even consultation) can be as beneficial as a cash contribution.

Government Officials
Local government officials, such as city councilpersons, state representatives, and even members of Congress have access to funds that may be available for neighborhood projects. They can also be important connectors who can help facilitate relationships between your group and grant-making organizations.

Liberty Lands Park: The Heart of a Neighborhood

Creating a fun, welcoming environment is important for any community garden, and Liberty Lands Park in the Northern Liberties section of Philadelphia serves as a great example. According to Janet Finegar, co-chair of the Northern Liberties Neighborhood Association, "The park has become the heart of the neighborhood, and there's a constant demand for garden plots."

Liberty Lands, which includes 36 community garden plots and a playground, holds events throughout the year. The most popular fundraiser is a biannual music festival, where local bands play free of charge and the relaxed atmosphere makes it feel more like a party. Liberty Lands also hosts movie nights, a variety show, flea markets, and a neighborhood house-and-garden tour.

These events not only help raise money for the site, but they also draw people from all over the neighborhood and other parts of the city, creating a huge interest in the garden and park. Liberty Lands has been integral in helping to transform the Northern Liberties neighborhood from an industrial area into the hotspot it is today. The park has contributed to the increase in nearby property values—adjacent condominiums even trumpet proximity to the park as a selling point.

Liberty Lands is owned and operated by a neighborhood organization (Northern Liberties Neighborhood Association) and the community. NLNA develops partnerships with other organizations and businesses and has been a key to the garden's longevity and success over the years.

Regular cleanup days and organizational meetings ensure that things run smoothly. The garden committee tries to make workdays pleasant by having doughnuts and coffee on hand, as well as sharing a potluck lunch after the work is done. And, Janet adds: "We do a lot of congratulating and thanking people for their work in addition to nagging them to do it."

The success of Liberty Lands stems in no small part from the strong commitment of the group, which is partly held together by a shared penchant for fun—not to mention doughnuts.

Obtaining Grants

For a well-established community garden, obtaining a grant from a foundation, business, or agency can be hugely helpful. But do your research! Grant-making organizations usually have specific areas of focus; make sure your project is a good fit.

The first step is learning about the corporations and industries in your area. Many big businesses have charitable foundations, so check their websites to see if they might offer grants that match your objective. Also browse your city's business journal, many of which publish a "Book of Lists" that identifies philanthropic organizations.

If you find a promising lead, write a proposal, follow the instructions precisely, and adhere to deadlines. Funders may eliminate proposals that do not meet their guidelines. Include supporting information, such as project costs, letters of recommendation in support of the project, and any publicity your garden has received.

Documentation and statistics help bolster your case. Consider the number of people who use the garden weekly, the pounds of produce grown, or any other figures that will illustrate the value of your efforts. Be clear about your goals for the garden and how, if applicable, they stand to benefit the community at large.

When submitting an application, make it look as professional as possible. See if someone in your group can create letterhead for your community garden. A website also adds legitimacy to your activities.

A National Resource for Grant Seekers
The Foundation Center (*http://foundationcenter.org*) is a national organization that maintains a comprehensive database of foundations all over the country. On its website, you can search by foundations' areas of interest. You can also view tax filings for particular foundations showing what grants they have made in past years.

Becoming a 501(c)(3)

Some gardens may decide to form a 501(c)(3), a federally recognized charitable organization. This comes with many benefits, particularly making garden-related expenses tax exempt. But navigating bureaucracy can be intimidating and the process can be costly. Only well-established gardens that are serious about soliciting donations and are capable of providing a pubic service should consider this option.

An alternative is partnering with an existing organization that already has 501(c)(3) status, such as a neighborhood civic association. By stepping under that organization's "umbrella," you may have to concede some control over decision-making and allocation of funds. On the plus side, the affiliation helps forge your group's identity and purpose while sharing responsibilities and resources.

Understanding the Value of Volunteers

Remember that time has a value too. Although the work of maintaining a community garden falls to the gardeners, there may be times when the group needs a little outside help. If you need volunteers for a big task, be strategic. Most schools have a service-learning requirement, and you may be able to work with a teacher to have an entire class come out to lend a hand. Or perhaps a local religious institution would devote a service day to the garden. Before the project begins, be clear about volunteer roles.

Volunteers are potential gardeners, so let them know a bit about your garden and share information about membership. If nothing else, recognize that their time and effort is valuable and express your gratitude.

Generating Good Will & Having Fun

Running a community garden takes commitment and effort. So make time to have fun as a group as well. Garden parties and events bring everyone together, celebrate the group's accomplishments, and build friendships.

Begin with a simple event like a potluck dinner. When hosting an event, be mindful of your fellow gardeners' labors and be sure guests are respectful of people's plots. This is especially relevant if non-gardeners will be in attendance.

Some favorite festivities include:
• Potlucks, picnics, and barbeques
• Parties for the summer solstice, harvest season, or holidays
• Competitions (e.g., entering a garden contest)
• Flea markets, yard sales, and plant swaps

Garden events can also be educational. Take advantage of your shared interests by having workshops or presentations on harvesting fall crops, canning and preserving, or preparing the beds for winter. Workshops are a great way to keep the group engaged during the winter months. Ask around to see who might be a good presenter.

Once gardeners start bonding over gardening, they tend to find other common interests as well. Don't be surprised if your community garden spawns a new knitting circle, book club, or babysitting co-op. A garden in which the people know each other and spend time together is one that will flourish for years to come. ▮

Chapter 3: Planning Your Community Garden

Finding a Garden Site

Now that you have a group of interested gardeners, all you need is a place to garden. Look around your neighborhood for an unused plot of land. Perhaps there is an abandoned vacant lot or part of a landscape around a community center, school, or faith-based institution. The garden site should be within walking distance or a short drive away from the people who are most likely to participate in the garden project. Ideally, the plot should receive at least six to eight hours of direct sunshine each day, be relatively flat, and be free of large debris or paved surfaces.

Agreement for Community Gardening

Name of gardener _____
Address _____
City, State, Zip _____
Telephone _____
Email _____
Date _____

Owner name _____
Address _____
City, State, Zip _____

Dear Mr./Ms. _____

According to city records, you are the listed owner of the property at

_____.

Residents of the surrounding community request permission to use this lot as a community garden. The gardeners agree to keep the lot clean and weed-free according to municipal regulations.

The gardeners agree to hold you harmless from and against any damage, loss, liability, claim, demand, suit, or expense directly or indirectly resulting from, arising out of, or in connection with the use of the garden by the garden group, its successors, assigns, agents and guests.

If you wish to sell or build on the lot in the future, the gardeners respectfully request that you notify them 60 days in advance of sale so they can remove plants and other gardening items.

This permission is for one (1) year and is automatically renewed each year unless the gardeners are notified otherwise in writing by you.

If you grant permission, please sign below and keep one copy for yourself and return the other to the gardening group at the address above.

_____   _____
Signature   Date

_____
Name

Getting Permission to Use a Vacant Lot

If you have spotted a potential garden site but don't know who owns the land, your first step is to try to determine ownership and get permission to use it. First you'll need the exact address. A vacant lot has the same address as any building that once occupied the site. Write down the addresses of adjacent properties; this will make it easier to verify the address of your site.

In many cases, municipalities make property data available online. Check the official government website for your city or town. If you can't find it online, take the address information to your local tax assessor's office, where ownership records should be on file.

Once you have the landowner's name and mailing address, write a letter using registered mail and request a return receipt. The letter should:

- request written permission to use the land for a community garden;
- ask for a term of one year with an option to renew;
- explain the value of the garden to the neighborhood and the fact that the gardeners will be responsible for upkeep of the site;
- and include a signature form for the landowner to sign and return to you.

The agreement should include a "Hold Harmless" waiver to assure the landowner that he or she will not be liable for any injuries or damage. In some cases, the landowner may ask you to purchase liability insurance (see page 35 for more on insurance).

If your letter is returned to you, save the returned mail as proof that you attempted to contact the owner. In many cases, vacant lots have been abandoned and owners cannot be located (or the owner may owe back taxes and doesn't want to be found). If your group decides to use a site without obtaining permission, keep in mind that you risk having the land taken away at any time if the owner should suddenly appear and want to sell or develop it.

In the case of delinquent landowners, the city or county government may have seized ownership of a property. In that case, find out which agency or department is responsible for the property and ask how to go about getting permission to use the site.

Although it's less common, some landowners may require a formal lease. Contact an attorney for help or draw up your own lease. Sample leases can be found on websites such as *www.Nolo.com*.

Sharing a Garden Site

Schools, churches, hospitals, or home-owners may be willing to let your group use part of their property for a garden—they may even want to participate. You should still obtain written permission and make sure that everyone is in agreement about the use of and responsibility for the garden.

Once you have secured permission to use a site, it's also a good idea to check with neighbors to make sure no one objects to a garden there. Circulate a survey letting people know that you plan to start a garden and asking for their name and an indication of support. It can be as simple as letting them check a box saying they are in favor of the garden or have no objections. Also ask if they may be interested in a garden plot.

Community Gardening Project Survey

Dear Neighbor:

A group of neighbors is starting a community garden at _____.
We are asking nearby residents to sign below to show that you support our efforts.

If you would like to participate in the garden, please check the box next to your name.
Thank you for your support.

Sincerely,
The Garden Committee

_____   _____   _____

_____   _____   _____

_____   _____   _____

Name	Address	Phone	Email	I'm interested in a plot

Connect With a Land Trust

Most people are familiar with rural and suburban land trusts that preserve farmland and open space to protect it from housing and commercial development pressures. In cities, community gardens in densely built environments face similar pressures.

These gardens are often created by residents in low- to moderate-income communities who transform formerly vacant, trash-filled lots into green oases. Typically the land is owned by private (sometimes tax-delinquent) owners or by the city.

In Philadelphia, many community gardeners have lost their gardens to development projects after years of caring for the land. The risk of losing more gardens led to the creation of the Neighborhood Gardens Association/A Philadelphia Land Trust (NGA). Incorporated in 1986, NGA is a nonprofit corporation whose mission is the long-term preservation of community-managed gardens and open spaces in Philadelphia.

A number of other cities have also formed community land trusts. New York City, Boston, Chicago, and Los Angeles have urban land trusts working to preserve green spaces that improve the quality of life in neighborhoods and complement other community development.

The steps vary from city to city and from one garden to another. In all cases it is important to research who owns the land that the community wants to protect. Then the garden group needs to determine if it wants to try to secure title to the land or negotiate a long-term lease. The group should then find out if a land trust or similar organization operates in their area and contact that organization for assistance.

If no such organization exists, you may decide to take on the challenge of establishing a new land trust. To do that, you will need to convene a board of directors, develop bylaws, and incorporate as a nonprofit organization. Land trusts must carry liability insurance on their properties and pay real-estate taxes or file for tax exemption. More details on starting a land trust can be found at NGA's website, *www.ngalandtrust.org*.

To find a land trust organization in your region, visit the website of the Land Trust Alliance, which represents 1,600 land trusts across the United States (*www.landtrustalliance.org*).

Finding Resources for Your Garden

The 360-Degree Community Asset Scan

A 360-degree sidewalk survey of your garden site will help identify potential assets for your garden. Facing the lot, describe what you see. Turn a few degrees to the right. Keep turning until you have a panoramic view of the immediate neighborhood, each time asking questions such as:

- Are houses being renovated or torn down nearby; could there be discarded bricks, blocks, or wood for paths, fences, or raised beds?

- Is the site near a city composting facility?

- Is there a tree-trimming crew operating in the area that may be willing to drop off wood chips?

- When is trash collected on the block?

- Is there a neighbor who sits on their front stoop who could keep an eye on things, perhaps in exchange for veggies?

- Is there a block captain or neighborhood organization?

- What businesses are nearby, and how can you involve them in the garden?

- What organizations are active in the neighborhood?

Conducting a Site Analysis

Use the information above to help complete an analysis of the garden site. This will help the group devise a realistic plan for the garden and agree on how to divide the space according to the activities that will take place in the garden.

Site Analysis for Garden Planning

What are the dimensions of the lot?

Length _____

Width _____

Area (length x width) _____

Irregular shape? _____

What kinds of plants do you want to grow in the garden?
(Check all that apply)
- ❐ Vegetables
- ❐ Flowers
- ❐ Herbs
- ❐ Fruit
- ❐ Shrubs
- ❐ Trees

Who will use the garden site? (Check all that apply)
- ❐ Adults
- ❐ Seniors
- ❐ Children/Youth
- ❐ Groups

What's the soil like?
- ❐ Will use soil already in the garden
- ❐ Will need to bring in compost
- ❐ Soil is hard and compacted, no weeds are growing
- ❐ Water puddles on soil surface
- ❐ We want to test the soil
- ❐ Other

Where will we get water for the garden?
- ❐ From a house (list address) _____
- ❐ From public housing (list address) _____
- ❐ From a fire hydrant

The closest working hydrant is: _____

Is it locked? Have you applied for a permit? _____

Will you store water in containers in the garden? _____

Will you use water barrels? _____

Other sources of water _____

Is the garden site sunny or shady?
- ❐ Full sun: 6 to 8 hours of direct sun each day
- ❐ Partial sun: at least 4 hours of direct sun each day
- ❐ Shady: not much sun at all
- ❐ Mixed: different parts get different amounts of sun

Is the garden surface flat or sloped?
- ❐ Flat, level
- ❐ Sloped
- ❐ Surface slopes toward walls/perimeter
- ❐ Rainwater runs out onto sidewalk
- ❐ There are paved surfaces in the lot
- ❐ We'd like to add different levels to the garden

Other _____

Dig up the "dirt" on your site. What is the history?
Talk to some of the older residents of the block about your site.

How long has it been vacant? _____

What used to be on the site? _____

Was it ever a factory or a gas station? _____

Are the adjacent houses occupied? _____

Are there walls around the site and what is their condition?

_____

Is the garden near a busy street or a factory? _____

Which side of the garden faces the most neighbors? _____

Describe the condition of adjacent house(s). Are any adjacent
houses vacant? _____

Is there anything on the lot that needs to be removed?

Trash _____

Weeds _____

Trees _____

Cement _____

Cars _____

Rocks & rubble _____

Other _____

Are there problem areas? (blacktop, muddy spots, tree stumps,
etc.)_____

Draw a map of the site
Start by drawing the shape of the site, measure the length of
each side of the site in feet, and note these measurements on
the drawing. Make sure the drawing includes the following:

- The exact address(es)
- All surrounding streets
- Available water source
- Existing fencing, walls, alleys, paths
- Problem areas (e.g. blacktop, muddy spots)
- Existing trees and shrubs—are they alive or dead?
- Put an E for east, where the sun rises
- Best location for a 10-foot delivery gate

Where is the Water?

When starting a new community garden, one of the most important early tasks is finding a way to get water to the site. Gardeners do this in various ways.

Many small community gardens work out an arrangement with a garden member or supporter who owns a home near the garden. The garden group reimburses the homeowner for the cost of water used in the garden, estimating the cost by comparing invoices to the homeowner's typical pre-garden water bill.

Check with your municipal water utility to see if there is a program for community gardens. In Philadelphia, the Philadelphia Water Department (PWD) offers a special program for community gardeners. The PWD provides a locked box that allows gardeners to use the nearest fire hydrant with a special tool to open the hydrant— most of which are capped to prevent residents from tampering with them. The box also contains a back-flow preventer and a meter. The Water Department monitors usage and picks up the box at the end of the gardening season. Currently there is no charge for this service. If there is a hydrant nearby without a cap, Philadelphia gardeners can apply for a permit to use the hydrant during the growing season to fill large food-grade barrels to store water on the garden site. (Note: open barrels should be covered with netting to prevent mosquitoes from hatching their eggs on the water's surface.) See page 78 for more on rain barrels.

Alternatively, gardeners can raise funds to hire a professional plumber, who can get necessary city permits and tap into the underground water supply, run a pipe directly to the garden, and install a tap. Typical costs run about $5,000 to $6,000. Your water utility may require that gardens be approved for this service by a legitimate third party, such as a neighborhood civic organization or social service agency.

Another option is for the garden to partner with a local civic association or nonprofit organization, which may qualify the garden for reduced rates for water purchased from the local utility.

Some community gardeners even strike up a relationship with the local fire station. Trucks sometimes come back from fire calls with water still in their pumpers, and fire fighters may be willing to discharge their water into reservoirs in the garden.

Whichever method your garden group chooses, good conservation practices will reduce water usage and expense. These include using soil rich in organic matter, which readily absorbs and retains water; covering planting beds with a two-inch layer of mulch to prevent drying out; and avoiding watering during the heat of the day.

Finally, establishing a water source is only part of the story. You will also need a system for delivering water to all the garden plots, which can be challenging for very large gardens. One method is to use hoses, pipes, or polypropylene flexible tubing buried 6 to 8 inches deep, with junction boxes every 50 feet or so, allowing individual gardeners to connect their own hoses.

quick tip

Check with your municipality's water utility to see if a program exists to provide water for community gardens. If not, see how you can help initiate one yourself!

Soil Smarts

Soil Preparation

Creating a new garden bed is heavy work. There are a few ways to tackle this job, but some are more difficult than others:

> **Not so easy:** Digging new beds directly in the ground with a shovel
> **Easier:** Digging beds using a gas-powered roto-tiller
> **Easiest:** Building raised beds on top of the ground

You'll want to remove any large debris, rocks, or big roots from the soil. Also, if you're digging in the ground, find out where the power, gas, sewer, and water lines enter the site. Most states have a "one call" system to help homeowners, contractors, and gardeners determine what's underground. (In Pennsylvania, call 811 or visit *www.pa1call.org*.)

A soil test will tell you the type of soil you have, as well as its pH. This will guide your decisions on soil amendments. For example, if you have heavy clay soil, you'll want to add something to improve drainage, such as sand. Conversely, if you live in a coastal area and have fast-draining, sandy soil, you'll require more compost to add nutrition and water-retention to the soil. Various amendments can also adjust the pH, so your plants aren't subjected to incorrect levels of alkalinity or acidity.

Because of the possible presence of toxic residue such as lead and heavy metals in urban soils, it's a good idea to have the soil tested before growing edible plants. (In Philadelphia, PHS has done extensive testing for lead, and most sites have been below the EPA-recommended level.) To determine if your soil has a high lead content, you can order a standard soil test from your county extension office (*www.csrees.usda. gov/extension*).

In addition to measuring heavy metals, check the soil pH. If your soil is above 6.8 (slightly alkaline) it helps reduce the absorption of heavy metals by plants.

iStockphoto.com

If your soil is in fact high in lead or other pollutants, growing edible plants in a raised bed is a good solution. For 4 x 8-foot beds, use boards in lengths of 4 and 8 feet, and 8 to 10 inches wide. You can put a weed barrier in the bottom to cover the ground. See page 75 for more on raised beds. Do not use pressure-treated wood or railroad ties for raised beds, since these may leach chemical toxins, such as arsenic, into soil.

Alternatively, you might consider growing plants in containers using clean soil or compost. For more information, read the University of Minnesota Extension Service fact sheet, "Lead in the Home Garden and Urban Soil Environment" (*www.exten sion.umn.edu/distribution/horticulture/DG2543.html*).

Compost: Black Gold for the Garden
Screened compost is the best fertilizer for any garden. Made of decomposed organic matter (disease-free plants, uncooked vegetable scraps, leaves, manure, etc.), compost not only provides essential nutrients for plant growth, but it also improves soil texture and drainage, promotes healthy root development, and helps maintain proper pH balance. Compost also promotes the growth of microorganisms, which help plants get nutrients from the soil. Chemical fertilizers may boost plant growth but often kill soil microorganisms. Over time this decreases organic matter in the soil, making plants more susceptible to insects and disease.

Composting requires the commitment of all the gardeners, so be sure to post rules about proper composting practices. Having one or more compost bins in the garden makes it easy for everyone to participate. You can make your own compost bins with wood and wire mesh or concrete blocks. Tumbling composters and other commercially made composters are available at garden centers and online outlets. You can also make a "compost tea" by soaking compost in water.

There are a multitude of books and websites offering information about making and using compost. Please see the Resources section for more information.

Hansberry Garden and Nature Center: A Resource for All Ages

The corner of Wayne Avenue and Hansberry Street in Philadelphia's Germantown neighborhood was once a trash-filled lot until a group of neighbors decided to do something about it. So in 2002 they enrolled in the PHS Garden Tenders training program and transformed the empty lot into the Hansberry Garden and Nature Center.

Founder Dave Schogel explains, "Our mission is to promote awareness, understanding, and appreciation of nature, and to cultivate a sense of community and neighborliness. Our gardeners range from newborns to teenagers to seniors, as well as all races. Our diversity is something we take pride in."

Students from two local schools, John B. Kelly Elementary and St. Martin de Porres Elementary, visit frequently. Hansberry members have given the students tours of the garden for the past four years and have also helped plant trees and build raised beds in the schoolyards. The garden also offers after-school enrichment programs, including classes on such topics as hydroponics and water quality.

Hansberry's classes and workshops aren't limited to children. The garden provides workshops for adults, and members can attend free demonstrations on cooking the fresh vegetables they grow. The Hansberry group also partners with a nearby senior center, which holds its annual picnic in the garden. The group has formed a 501(c)(3), which enabled it to purchase an adjacent vacant lot and expand the garden site. (Please see page 49 for information on forming a 501(c)(3).)

Neighborhood events are a big focus as well. In addition to a Community Health Fair and pumpkin painting, plans include a film night around Halloween and an annual family fun day. Hansberry's monthly flea markets, where people can buy plants, baked goods, used books, and household items, are another big draw.

By integrating gardening and environmental education into the community and offering fun, educational activities that appeal to all generations, Hansberry Garden and Nature Center has become a treasured resource for its neighborhood.

Tools

In most community gardens, individual members purchase their own tools, though most find ways to share large equipment like roto-tillers. The group may decide to use garden dues or raise money to purchase equipment. Another option is to ask for donations from local hardware stores or garden centers. Many community gardens have a shared storage shed, which, because of the risk of loss or theft, is usually used to hold less-valuable or older tools.

Tool Care

Proper care will extend the life of garden tools. First and foremost: don't leave your tools out in the rain! To prevent rust and corrosion of metal tools, clean off soil residue, hose it off, and dry it with a rag. Tools with moving, mechanical metal parts need occasional oiling to lubricate the moving parts, and cutting tools—from loppers and hand pruners to shovel blades—need periodic sharpening. You can either buy a sharpening stone and learn to do this yourself, or ask at your local hardware store if they have a tool-sharpening service. Oiling and sharpening each year in spring or at the end of the season is a good practice.

iStockphoto.com

dreamstime.com

Essential Garden Tools:

Shovels

The shovel is the indispensable earth-lifting tool. You'll use it early in the season for soil turning and digging holes for new plants. Its sharp blade can also cut sub-soil roots or ferret out rocks buried in the soil. There are several different kinds of shovels:

- Round-point shovel—lifts large quantities of soil or stone and cuts roots
- Square-point shovel—handy for lifting soil, stone, or mulch off a flat surface
- Garden spade—good for digging straight, precise lines in the soil, such as edging

Hoes

This traditional tool opens up long, narrow furrows in the soil for sowing seeds or setting out transplants. However, hoes are also good for weeding, since they're very accurate and have sharp blades.

Gloves

If you are working in the garden, you'll inevitably deal with sharp objects such as thorns, rough bark, or tools. For safety, wear heavy-duty gloves to spare your hands from injury, as well as insect bites and soil-borne diseases. And if you're working with children, they should always wear gloves, too.

Forks

Essentially a shovel with a forked tip, these are great for digging and lifting. They are especially useful for picking up loose, irregular materials like mulch or hay, as well as quickly opening up the earth for new plants and trees.

Trowels

An essential hand tool, the trowel is meant for smaller jobs or for when you're working on your hands and knees. It's also great for when you want to work fast and dig lots of small holes for seeds, plants, or bulbs.

Loppers, pruners, and shears

Loppers and pruners are used for cutting branches and foliage. They come in every configuration from hand-held to long-handle versions, as well as "pole cutters" for cutting tree branches. Shears, meanwhile, are more suited to cutting back excessive foliage, such as shaping a shrub or cutting back the thinner, low branches of a tree that are becoming intrusive.

Hoses

Hoses come in a large variety of styles, from traditional straight to coiled to "soaker" hoses that slowly release water around plants for deep watering. You can also look into all sorts of hose holders, such as hand-cranked wheels and in-ground watering systems and rain barrels.

Wheelbarrows

Wheelbarrows are great for transporting large quantities of soil, mulch, compost—or anything you need to move around in the garden.

Saws

For the gardener, perhaps the most useful saw is the standard "bow saw," which can cut through large branches quickly and easily. There are also curved, Japanese hand saws that some gardeners prefer, as well as pole saws for removing branches up in trees.

With any saw or cutting tool, safety is of paramount concern. Chainsaws are for really big jobs, such as cutting down small to mid-sized trees, but their hazards include breaking chains and falling trees and branches. Wear safety goggles at all times and get training on how to properly operate this useful, but potentially dangerous family of tools.

fork

bow saw

garden spade

hand saw

wheelbarrow

hoe

trowel

loppers
shears
hand pruners

round-point shovel

Designing a Community Garden

Once you've secured the land and completed your site analysis, it's time to plan what the garden will look like. This section offers guidelines for designing the most common type of community garden—a community vegetable garden or combination food and flower garden.

Community garden designs are as varied as the neighborhoods where they are located, the size of the garden site, and the needs and ideas of the gardeners. However, whether the garden is tucked into a tiny row-house lot, takes up an entire city block, or sits on expansive parkland, the same basic considerations will help guide the design process.

First, make a wish list with all the activities and garden features your group wants to include on the site and note the space required for each element. Decide which things are possible right away and which may have to wait until the future, saving space for them to be added later. Some gardens contain ponds, potting sheds, and beehives—the possibilities are endless.

Consider whether you'd like to include any communal plots, such as a children's plot or a bed for vegetables to be donated to a food cupboard or homeless shelter. You may also want to set aside space for special crops maintained by the group.

The front or perimeter of the garden helps determine how your community will view the garden, so make sure it looks good. You may decide to plant flowering plants or evergreens at the entrance to create a pleasing appearance. Rows of tall sunflowers or vines growing on the fence are also good options.

Draw the Garden Plan

Plan the garden on paper first, using information from your site analysis, and include possible arrangements and spacing of plots. Take the base map you created. Lay tracing paper over it and start adding details from your wish list into the plan.

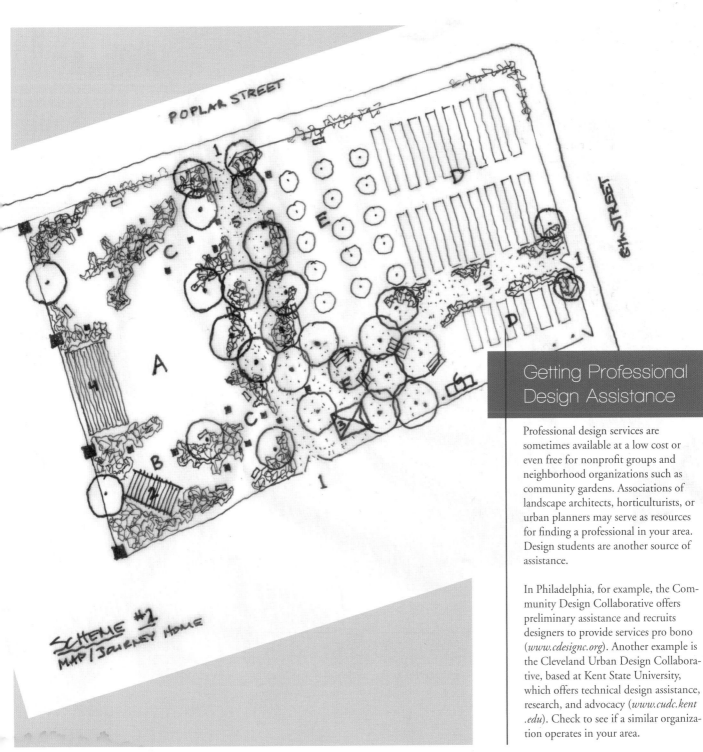

POPLAR STREET

6th STREET

SCHEME #2
MAP/JOURNEY HOME

Getting Professional Design Assistance

Professional design services are sometimes available at a low cost or even free for nonprofit groups and neighborhood organizations such as community gardens. Associations of landscape architects, horticulturists, or urban planners may serve as resources for finding a professional in your area. Design students are another source of assistance.

In Philadelphia, for example, the Community Design Collaborative offers preliminary assistance and recruits designers to provide services pro bono (*www.cdesignc.org*). Another example is the Cleveland Urban Design Collaborative, based at Kent State University, which offers technical design assistance, research, and advocacy (*www.cudc.kent .edu*). Check to see if a similar organization operates in your area.

Jimmy Asnes

Curtis "50 Cent" Jackson Community Garden: Form Meets Function

In 2007, the space formerly known as the Baisley Park Community Garden began its remarkable transformation into the Curtis "50 Cent" Jackson Community Garden. This 15,120-square-foot space in Queens, New York—situated on a corner lot bordered by an embankment and railroad tracks—was active for many years with vegetable growing, but was a plot sorely in need of a renaissance.

That feat has now been extraordinarily realized thanks to the partnership forged between New York Restoration Project (NYRP) and rap sensation Curtis "50 Cent" Jackson. Giving back to his childhood neighborhood and the community that has supported him over the years, Jackson joined forces with NYRP founder and entertainer Bette Midler—not for a duet, but to breathe new life into this much-needed green space. As a result, the surrounding area and the lives of local residents have blossomed right along with this revitalized community treasure.

Generously underwritten by 50 Cent's G-Unity Foundation, the site features the talents of acclaimed landscape architect and designer Walter Hood. For six months, NYRP's horticulture crews and design team worked side-by-side with Hood and local residents to realize the community's vision for the space. Incorporating vegetable plots and a patio area, the garden does much to draw the community into the garden and take the garden out into the community. An innovative and wildly creative design makes the property not only a lively, multi-functional gathering space, but also provides gardeners with amenities such as a unique rainwater harvesting system, composed of 10-foot-tall funnels, which provides regular irrigation, as well as shade for rest and relaxation.

Opened in November 2008, the renovated Curtis "50 Cent" Jackson Community Garden provides neighborhood residents with access to green space, where residents now have the opportunity to host educational and cultural events, gardening workshops, family activities, and much more.

Located in the Jamaica section of Queens, the garden represents a much-needed resource for an area that currently has less than five percent of the recommended amount of open space necessary to serve its more than 52,000 children residents.

For more information on the garden or NYRP, please visit *www.nyrp.org*.

Right Plant/Right Place

When selecting a plant, be sure you understand its characteristics.
- What is the plant's size at maturity, both height and width?
- What color are its flowers?
- What kind of bark or leaf texture does it have?
- Does the plant produce fruit or other droppings?
- Is the plant evergreen (holds its needles or leaves all year) or deciduous (drops needles or leaves in the autumn)?

Plants will thrive in the right environment. Learn what conditions the plant needs for healthy growth, and consider these factors when choosing a location.

Soil Conditions
Soil pH: indicates whether soil is acidic (lower than 7.0) or alkaline (higher than 7.0)
Fertility: available nutrients
Drainage: how the soil absorbs water
Compaction: hard, compacted soil, no space for air and water circulation or root growth
Pollutants: heavy metals that may inhibit plant growth

> *Solutions:* Test your soil for pH. Use lime to raise pH and sulfur to lower it. Work compost into the soil to increase fertility and improve drainage. If soil is excessively compacted or polluted, consider growing in raised beds. Note: In urban areas the soil often has a high pH due to bricks and mortar left on sites where buildings have been demolished. Test your soil before adding any lime.

Light Conditions
Full Sun: six to eight hours of direct sunlight per day
Partial shade/sun: sunny at only certain times of day
Shade: little or no direct sunlight

> *Solutions:* Plant shade-loving plants under a tree or in the shadow of a building or fence. Plant trees and shrubs to provide future shade. For more light, remove obstacles such as trees and large shrubs or branches; paint adjacent walls white to increase reflected light.

Site Exposure
Wind: strong winds that dry out plants and affect plant growth
Heat: excessive reflected heat from surrounding buildings or pavement

> *Solutions:* Provide shade. Create plant communities by grouping them together. Cut down on reflected light by covering the ground with mulch. Create a windbreak with a fence or hardy plants such as a row of shrubs or trees.

Raised beds provide good drainage, warm up earlier in spring, and clearly delineate garden plots.

Where to Plant: Sun and Shade

Your site analysis has identified the sunlight and shade patterns on the site during the growing season. When choosing the location of plots, place vegetables beds where they will get the most light. Put tall plants or trellises at the north side of the garden to avoid shading the vegetable plots.

Nearby buildings or trees may block sunlight. However, some shade may be desirable. Shady spots are good places for benches and sitting areas. If there is no shade on the site, you may want to plant trees or shrubs or build a gazebo. If your garden is in a windy location, you may need a windbreak to protect tender plans; you can plant a windbreak using fast-growing evergreens such as arborvitae, holly, or pine trees.

Raised beds

Growing in a raised bed with fresh soil or compost allows you to skip the process of soil testing. Raised beds also offer other benefits. They provide better drainage, warm up earlier in the spring, and clearly delineate garden plots. If you keep the width of the raised bed to four feet or less, you can work the bed from the edges, so it's easier to maintain, and you can place plants closer together, increasing your yield. Raised beds are also a good option for elderly gardeners or those with physical disabilities.

Generally, raised beds should be about 4 feet wide by 8 feet long and made with naturally rot-resistant wood (not chemically treated), or stones, concrete blocks, recycled-plastic lumber, or other inert, sturdy materials. The framing material should be 6 to 12 inches above ground, and extend at least 4 inches below ground. Fill the bed with high-quality screened compost or a mixture of compost and topsoil.

Raised beds are simple to build; sample designs can be found online or in many gardening books. Please see the Resources section for more information.

Containers

Nearly any plant grown in the ground can also be grown in a container. Containers may be desirable for certain plants that spread too quickly (such as mint), for children or elderly gardeners, or for tender plants that need to be moved indoors during the winter (such as citrus trees). Keep in mind that containers dry out much more quickly than garden soil, so they need frequent watering, as much as every day during hot weather. If you want to have containers, make sure someone is available to check and water them frequently.

Eileen Gallagher

Garden Structures

Every garden should include space for shared materials like compost and woodchips. If you decide to put a fence around the garden, include a 10-foot-wide gate for delivery of bulk materials. Other optional structures include:

Benches

Everyone needs to take a break now and then, so don't forget to include a place to sit. You needn't spend a lot of money on benches; used ones can often be found at garage sales and flea markets.

Compost bins

Set aside space for compost bins where they will be accessible to all gardeners.

Gazebo

A gazebo is an ideal place for garden meetings, welcoming visitors to the garden, or just relaxing.

Storage and work sheds

Many community gardens have storage sheds that allow members to conveniently share tools or materials. A word of caution about sheds: if your garden is located where theft or vandalism could be a problem, a locked storage shed may invite trouble, as it tells the world there is something inside worth stealing. Another option is an open work shed with low-value items such as extra gloves, hoses, and watering cans.

Bulletin boards

Rain-proof or covered message boards or signs are handy for posting garden rules and meeting dates.

Common-Use Areas

Decide what type of common-use areas or shared structures to include in the garden. Obviously, the larger the garden, the more options you have for these additions.

Gathering spaces

Setting aside part of the garden for common use makes it easy for gardeners to socialize and have fun. Something as simple as a picnic table for potluck dinners will bring the group together. Be sure to include language in your bylaws that spells out how the group will share responsibility for these areas. Other possibilities include:

- Tables and chairs
- Barbecue grill
- Sitting garden
- Play area or children's garden
- Meadow
- Pond
- Shade structure or small tree

Communal crops

For crops that require a lot of space, gardeners may decide to create a special section of the garden where they can care for these plants together. Or you may want to set aside one or more vegetable plots that the gardeners tend collectively, such as a plot to grow food for donation to a food bank. If the garden group includes families with young children, you might want a special children's plot (see Chapter 5). Typical communal crops include:

- Berry patch
- Grape arbor
- Children's garden
- Herb garden
- Fruit trees or small orchard
- Trees for shady sitting areas
- Pumpkin patch
- Cutting garden or wildflower meadow
- Raised bed for elderly or disabled gardeners or visitors
- Perennial beds

Greening your Garden

Composting

Why bag your garden waste and send it to the landfill when you can turn it into a rich fertilizer that improves your soil better than any chemical additive? See page 63 for more on compost.

Rain barrels

A rain barrel lets you collect water for use in the garden, free of charge. You may be able to connect the rain barrel to a downspout on an adjacent building (with permission, of course) or on the roof of a garden shed or gazebo. Rain barrels not only provide free water, but they also benefit the surrounding environment by collecting storm runoff that may contribute to flooding and pollution. Visit the PHS website's YouTube page (*www.PHSonline.org*) for a video on making your own rain barrel.

Solar panels

Solar panels installed on the roofs of structures provide cheap power for operating lights, water pumps, and other garden features.

Welcoming beneficial creatures

Bats

Bat houses are simple to build, and bats consume huge numbers of mosquitoes, making gardening more pleasant.

Bees

Many well-established community gardens have beehives. Bees pollinate food-producing plants, and the group can use the honey or sell it to raise funds for the garden.

Birds

Birdhouses are another nice addition, as are plants that attract hummingbirds.

See the Resources section for more on welcoming wildlife to the garden.

What is Edible Landscaping?

Although both the concept and practice of edible landscaping are ancient, the term may be unfamiliar to today's gardeners. Edible landscaping merges the functionality of growing food with the aesthetic qualities of ornamental gardening. In essence, it's the act of planting trees, shrubs and herbaceous plants that bring us fruits, nuts, and vegetables to eat, along with joy and pleasure for our senses.

Edible landscaping goes a step beyond annual vegetable gardening. Instead of just fresh tomatoes, peppers, and beans in summer, edible landscaping provides an array of food, from spring fruit to early winter nuts. In fact, it minimizes the need for annual plantings, since it makes use of trees, shrubs, and perennial plants.

The reasons for food gardening are many, including having fresher, safer, better-tasting food; saving money by eating home-grown food; teaching children about healthy eating habits; and growing specialty foods not easily found in stores. Having a beautiful landscape along with a bounty of food combines the best of both worlds.

Edible landscaping relies on the same basic principles and steps as any landscaping or gardening project.

First, walk around the garden site and determine:
- Available space—locate and measure large open areas, small edges, corners, or patches
- Amount of sunshine—most edibles need a minimum of six hours daily
- Noticeably wet or dry soils—some edibles like these extremes but most prefer well-drained soil
- Quality of soil and evidence of contamination—always test soil before starting a new garden.

Second, think about what you like to eat and then find out if it will grow in your community garden, taking into account the specific requirements of each plant. For example, raspberry bushes need sun and well-drained soil, but blueberry bushes like some moisture and shade. Walnut trees grow very large, up to 40 or 60 feet high by 25 to 30 feet wide, and the roots emit a tannin that is toxic to lots of other edibles, so they require lots of space.

Lastly, identify your goals and approach. If you have the space and commitment, you can grow a full-year's food supply. Or, you may simply want to enjoy in-season fresh-picked foods in spring, summer, and fall, integrating edible plants into the overall garden plan. Either way, start small and simple and clarify your group's future goals as you go along.

A few additional facts and suggestions:
- Be prepared: most edible plants attract birds, bees, and other wildlife.
- Be smart: dwarf fruit and nut trees are easier to pick and don't interfere with utilities.
- Be creative and have fun: express your personal style, whether formal, fun, or funky.

See the Resources section for more information on edible landscaping. ∎

Chapter 4: Plants, Tools & Tips

Choosing What to Grow

Now that you've formed a great group, secured a garden site, prepared the soil, and created a garden plan, it's time to think about the fun stuff—plants!

First, you'll need to figure out which plants will grow best in your climate. As Barbara Damrosch notes in her book, *The Garden Primer*, "Each region has a set of vegetables that are easier to grow than others. Southerners have no trouble with okra, sweet potatoes, eggplant and peanuts. Northerners have an easy time with cool-weather crops such as broccoli, peas, lettuce, and cabbage (as do Southerners if they wait for cool weather). Gardeners in wet climates excel at celery; those in dry ones succeed with sweet potatoes."

While this section discusses some of the most widely grown crops, talk to other gardeners, your local County Extension Service, or browse online sources to see which plants grow best in your area. You can also find out when to plant for your area from these sources. Also, determine which gardening USDA Hardiness Zone your garden is in. (*www.usna.usda.gov/Hardzone/ushzmap.html*)

When to Plant

In basic terms, vegetable crops fall into two groups: those that thrive in cool weather and those that should not be planted until after the last frost. In most parts of the country, early crops include greens such as lettuce, spinach, Swiss chard, and mustard, as well as peas, onions, beets, and cole crops (broccoli and cabbage). Some herbs, such as dill, also grow best in cool periods, so sow it directly outside early in your region's growing season, then again toward the end.

Wait until after the last projected frost date to plant warm-weather crops such as tomatoes, eggplant, peppers, and tender herbs such as basil. However, if you live in a city, where the soil warms up more quickly, you can plant 10 to 15 days earlier than those who live in less protected locations. (If you're in a low-lying area or "frost pocket," you may need to wait until later.)

Seed Starting and Planting

A time-honored way to get your plants is to start them from seed, but not all plants are as conducive to seed-starting as others. You can break down your plant planning like this:

- Seeds sown directly in the ground before the last frost (peas, lettuce, beets, spinach, turnips)
- Seeds sown directly in the ground after the last frost (corn, beans, squash, basil)
- Seeds started indoors in soil-less mix (tomatoes, cauliflower, celery, cabbage)
- Pre-grown plant "starts" bought at a nursery or plant sale (tomatoes and peppers)

iStockphoto.com

Starting Seeds Indoors

For warm-weather plants, you need to start them indoors and transplant them to the garden after the last frost. Plant them in sterilized seed-starting mixture (also known as a "soil-less mix"). You can buy seed-starting trays at your local nursery or online, but you can also make your own—anything that holds a medium will work, provided you can easily place it where it will receive ample light. On top, you can put a clear plastic lid (store-bought trays often come with their own) or plastic kitchen wrap, as long as you punch a few holes in it for air circulation. At the very beginning you don't need much circulation, but as the seeds begin to sprout, you'll want to open up air slots to prevent fungal outbreaks that can easily kill the seedlings.

Start basil seeds inside for transplanting outdoors after the last frost. Sow seeds of tomatoes, peppers, peas, and eggplants in seed trays, place in a bright area where soil-less mix will remain between 70° and 75° F, and cover with plastic to retain moisture to encourage germination. Once your seedlings have germinated, move them to cooler temperatures for sturdy growth.

quick tip: hardening off

Be sure to harden off the plants before setting them out—this is the process of slowly acclimating indoor seedlings to the harsher outdoor environment. Put tender plants and seedlings outside during the day and bring them back inside at night. You can also use a cold frame for hardening off or set the containers in a protected area and cover them with light plastic row or cover fabric.

Starting Seeds Outdoors

Outside, snaps peas are one of the earliest seeds to sow in the vegetable garden. Once the weather begins to warm up, you can also plant potatoes, onion sets, and onion plants outdoors. Also good to set out early are lettuce and spinach. Put transplants of cabbage and broccoli into the garden for early yield before the weather gets warm. After planting, surround each seedling with a small collar (one to two inches deep) to deter cutworms from severing the stem. Look around for discarded objects to reuse for this purpose, such as paper cups from which you can remove the bottom.

Hardy herbs (sage, mint, tarragon, and chives) should be planted into the garden earlier in the season, or in the fall. If you need only a couple of plants, you probably will find it more practical to buy plants of these herbs, rather than sowing them from seed. Mint is invasive, so plant it where it cannot spread over less vigorous plants, or grow it in a container.

quick tip: mini hothouses

Collect milk jugs and cartons to use as mini-hothouses to protect the early seedlings as you move them from the house or cold frame to open garden.

iStockphoto.com

Purchasing Plants

Once your area is past frost, you can go shopping for plants. Look for tight, compact plants with dark green leaves throughout (passing up those with yellowing leaves or elongated stems); check under leaves for aphids and white-flies.

If you order plants by mail, open the boxes when they arrive to check them. Most plants are shipped in a dormant state, so don't worry if the foliage is brown and dead or if the roots look limp; in some cases, you'll see dormant buds in the center of the plant. If you intend to plant within a few days, rewrap the plants in moist (not soggy) packing material and leave them in a cool, dimly lit place. But if the weather or soil conditions will not allow planting for a longer period, place the plants into a shallow trench and cover the roots with a mixture of equal parts sand and compost.

Do not transplant in the heat of the day. Wait until evening and shield new plantings from the hot sun for a day or two with bushel baskets or pots. Separate tangled root systems by gently pulling roots apart and water seedlings well.

iStockphoto.com

Intensive Gardening

Intensive gardening is all about getting the maximum yield of produce from a smaller area. Instead of having long rows of crops, an intensive garden wastes no space and has plants growing in every part of the garden all season long. A related approach is succession planting, in which two or more crops of the same plant are grown in succession, or when plants with different maturity dates are grown together. Nutrient-rich, organic compost is the key to this type of gardening. Intensive gardens aren't just terrestrial—vertical gardening up trellises and fences is another way to maximize yields.

iStockphoto.com

Tomatoes: Space tomatoes four feet apart, while peppers and eggplants can be planted more closely. Mix compost into the soil at the base of each planting hole. Plant tomato seedlings deeply, covering the stems beyond the pair of leaves closest to the roots. Remove this set of leaves before planting. Additional roots will form at leaf nodes. Assemble the stakes or cages that you're going to use to support them—it's easiest to put these in as you install the plants.

Eggplants & Peppers: Plant eggplants and peppers at the same depth as in the seedling container. Surround each plant with a cutworm collar made from a strip of cardboard or plastic.

Cucumbers: Cucumbers flourish in hot, humid weather and rich soil. Prepare your cucumber planting bed by adding manure (aged from the barnyard if you can get hold of it, or dried cow manure from the garden center). To warm the soil for cucumbers, melons, and other heat-loving crops, some gardeners cover it with black plastic, and then plant the seedlings through slits in the plastic.

Garden Maintenance

Watering

Watering your plants deeply once a week, or twice a week in hot summer weather, is better than giving the garden a short sprinkle every day. Water slowly and gently, directing water to the roots of plants. It's best to water in the morning, as it allows time for the leaves to dry during the day, which can prevent fungal diseases.

Weed Control

With the garden come the weeds. Turn your back on a planting area for a couple of weeks and you will surely find it full of invaders. Weeds compete with plants for water, nutrients, space, and light.

Weeding by hand and hoe are old and effective methods. Pull by hand when the ground is damp so you get as much of the roots as possible. If you use a hoe, do it before a couple of dry days so pulled weeds will wither and die rather than re-root.

Mulching

Mulching is a wonderful way to control weeds. Mulch is anything that covers the soil to warm it up, cool it off, keep it moist, and keep weeds from growing. Newspaper, salt hay, shredded hardwood, grass clippings, or leaves are all good mulches. Mulch not only helps keep weed seeds from sprouting, but it also adds organic matter to improve soil structure. Spread a two-inch layer of mulch. On shrub beds and under trees, woodchips or pine bark are appropriate. In the vegetable garden, grass clippings, salt hay, composted leaves, and even newspapers or black plastic are good choices. If your mulch supply is short, you can start with a layer of newspaper, then put the leaves on top.

Nadine Ford

Little Sugar Creek Greenway Community Garden: A Classroom for All

If a resident of Mecklenburg County, in North Carolina, wants to learn about composting or organic gardening, a good place to start is the Little Sugar Creek Greenway Community Garden. Created as a compost demonstration site, Little Sugar Creek has it all—from traditional "hot pile" composting and passive composting (throw it on a pile and let it sit) to the lasagna method (layering), worm composting, and trench composting (more on that later).

Located about two miles from downtown Charlotte, NC, the garden is situated on a floodplain on county-owned land. An abandoned community garden on the site was renovated in 2009 with help from the Charlotte Bobcats basketball team and Johnson & Wales University College of Culinary Arts.

Little Sugar Creek serves as a teaching facility and community resource and is supported by a partnership between the LUESA Mecklenburg County Organic Waste Reduction program; Keep Mecklenburg Beautiful (an affiliate of Keep America Beautiful, a national beautification and waste reduction program); and the Mecklenburg County Park and Recreation Department.

Nadine Ford, a senior environmental specialist with the LUESA program, manages the garden education programs and tests various organic gardening and composting methods. She says trench composting is great for beginners. With this method the gardener first puts a row of plants into the ground without improving the soil, then digs a trench next to that row and adds organic waste matter, covering it with soil. The following year, the gardener puts next year's crop into the composted trench. Row by row over time, the soil of the entire garden is improved with compost.

"This is an area with a lot of clay soil," says Ford, "and people get discouraged, so this helps them get started quickly and also teaches them about crop rotation."

Ford is also experimenting with "bokashi" composting. This intensive composting technique uses a closed bin and a "starter culture" made from anaerobic microorganisms (known as "effective microorganisms" or EM), which are typically mixed with molasses, water, and wheat bran.

Because Little Sugar Creek is an educational facility, there are no individual plots. Instead, the garden is open to anyone who wants to come in and help tend it or learn about gardening. The fresh food grown there is available to anyone, too, not just those in the surrounding neighborhood.

Ford offers classes for adults and children throughout the year. Another project involves prison inmates through a partnership with the Mecklenburg County Sheriff's Office. The inmates grow seeds (provided by Keep Mecklenburg Beautiful) in a prison greenhouse and the seedlings are planted at Little Sugar Creek, as well as distributed to school gardens and other community gardens in the county.

An expansion project in 2010 earned the garden special recognition from the Scotts Miracle-Gro "Give Back to Grow" program and Keep America Beautiful.

Harvesting

Every vegetable gardener gets to a point in summer where harvesting becomes the name of the game, but it's important to know the right time to harvest your crops. If you pick too soon, the food may not be fully ripe and may not have developed its full flavor and nutritional punch. On the other hand, leaving crops on the plant too long can invite bug infestation, disease, and animal scavengers. Many garden books and websites provide harvesting guidelines for specific plants, as well as tips on using, storing, and preserving your bounty of fresh produce.

Fall Cleanup

Unless you are growing fall and/or winter crops (see "Extending the Season" on page 101), fall is the time to clean out the vegetable garden and replenish the soil.

Remove spent plants, stems, and weeds without seeds and put them in the composter. However, place diseased or bug-infested plants and weeds with seeds in a plastic bag and put them in the trash—not in the compost pile, where they may survive and infest your garden next year.

Add organic matter such as compost, manure, or shredded leaves and work it into the soil. You may want to plant a cover crop, also known as "green manure," to add nitrogen and organic matter and help stop erosion (see page 101 for more on cover crops).

Prune any dead, diseased, damaged, or crossing branches on trees. Replenish mulch around perennials, trees, and shrubs. Fall is also a great time to plant new hardy perennials, because it gives their roots time to establish and get a head start on spring growth.

Make a Garden Calendar

Between mulching, weeding, pruning, and planning, there's a lot
for a community gardener to keep track of! Simplify things by
making a calendar. The calendar should include everyday activities,
large-scale events, and everything in between, such as:

- Deadlines for new-gardener applications, leadership
  nominations, and paying dues.
- Meetings, even if they are regularly occurring it helps to have
  reminders.
- Special occasions, including holidays, picnics, parties,
  school-group visits, and the like.
- Workdays and other garden-wide efforts.
- Outside events. Use the calendar to spread the word about
  farmers markets, street fairs, garden contests, or anything
  else that might interest your fellow gardeners.
- Seasonal chores, including harvest days, fall cleanup, and
  spring workdays.
- Horticultural happenings. Share advice about when to
  purchase seeds, plant peas, or aerate the soil.

Although you can draft, print, and distribute a paper version of the
calendar, this might be the perfect project for one of the more Web-
minded members of your group. An online calendar is interactive,
allowing for multiple contributors and editing and updating as
needed.

quick tip

Don't add weeds with seeds to your compost pile, since weed seeds may survive in the compost and sprout in your garden when you use the compost.

Cover Crops

The concept of cover crops is quite simple and, indeed, quite ancient. The idea is to plant a "nutritious" crop during the off-season, usually fall and winter, to add nitrogen and other beneficial elements to the soil. Cover crops vary depending on your location, but winter rye, buckwheat, and various members of the legume family are the most commonly used. Contact your local County Extension service (*www.csrees.usda.gov /extension*), talk to other gardeners, or search online to find the best plants for your area.

Some gardeners strongly believe in this technique, while others prefer to simply garden all year long with harvestable winter plants. For more on cover crops visit *www.attra.ncat.org*.

Extending the Season

While you are harvesting your bountiful summer crops, turn your thoughts ahead to fall. Most gardeners practice warm-season gardening, which includes everything that is not frost-tolerant. However, gardening doesn't have to end with the first autumn frost—or wait for the warm temperatures of May and June in spring; it can stretch into the winter.

Cool-season gardening includes many crops that don't appreciate hot summer temperatures. These include root crops such as carrots, beets, turnips, radishes, and potatoes; leafy crops like lettuces, mustard, turnips, spinach, kale, and collards; and cole crops (also known as crucifers), which include broccoli, broccoli rabe, Brussels sprouts, cabbage, and cauliflower.

Plant fall crops in late summer; many vegetables will have up to 90 days to mature during the cooler days of fall. Plant seeds a little deeper than you would in the spring, since the ground dries out faster in the summer sun. Keep a close watch and don't let seedlings dry out. As in spring, soil preparation is important. Spring and summer crops have been steadily draining nutrients from the soil, and you need to replace these nutrients if fall crops are to do well. Dig in plenty of compost or rotted manure.

quick tip

If you want to plant crops in autumn, remember to buy seeds for cool-season crops in the winter or spring, since garden centers may run out by late summer.

Row cover fabric or floating row covers shield plants from pests and frost while letting in sunlight, water, and air. This extends the early and late season, provides frost protection down to 28°F, and aids in germination by keeping soil moist. Row cover fabric comes in various weights.

iStockphoto.com

Using a Cold Frame or Hoop House

You can extend the growing season even further with the help of a cold frame or a hoop house (a simple greenhouse made of PVC piping and plastic sheeting). These inexpensive, simple structures protect tender plants from freezing temperatures and precipitation. Cold frames are especially simple to make. Hoop house kits are available from many online retailers, but you can also make your own.

Trees and Shrubs

If your community garden will include trees or shrubs, decide which kind of woody plant is most appropriate for the site. Consider overhead wires, amount of sunlight, soil pH, and drainage. Each woody plant species has specific requirements, and some are more tolerant of environmental stresses like road salts, compacted soil, and air pollution. Knowing your site will help you choose a tree that will thrive.

Ask yourself if the tree or shrub will be appropriate in 25 years. Imagine each plant in a planting site when it reaches its mature size. Can the site accommodate a large shrub or tree? Would a small tree, a columnar tree, or a large shrub suit the site better? Does the plant produce seeds, cones, or other droppings that might pose a problem in the garden? Allow adequate spacing between plants based on their size at maturity. And for new tree plantings, select at least 2 ½-inch-caliper trees (the diameter of the trunk), since these are not as easily damaged as smaller saplings.

Water

Newly planted trees and shrubs require one inch of rain per week or equivalent supplemental watering during the first two years after planting. Be sure you have a plan in place to provide adequate water. When watering, the golden rule is "water weekly and deeply." Allow 10 to 15 gallons of water to seep slowly; watering too

fast will cause the water to flow off the planting site. It's best to use a trickling hose or five-gallon bucket with holes. You can also use a Treegator®, a large plastic bag that zips around the tree trunk. When filled, it delivers water slowly and evenly directly to the root system of a newly planted tree with no run-off or evaporation. Discontinue watering when the ground freezes. Start again in the spring when tree buds swell and sprout new leaves.

Mulch

Use mulch around trees and shrubs to conserve moisture and discourage weeds. Apply mulch evenly at a depth of two inches. Do not pile mulch around the trunks of trees or shrubs because it traps moisture and encourages disease. Keep mulch at least two to three inches away from trunks and woody stems (the mulch layer should look more like a donut than a mountain). PHS recommends double-shredded hardwood mulch, dark brown. Rake and replenish mulch annually.

Pruning

Tree pruning falls into two categories: Major tree pruning involves removing large branches from mature trees, as well as tree removal. Pruning tree branches beyond the reach of a hand-held pole pruner requires a professional. If you need to find a professional arborist, visit the website of the International Society of Arboriculture (*www.isa-arbor.com*). Ask for credentials, insurance verification, and references, and choose the contractor in whom you have the most confidence.

Minor tree pruning is removing dead, damaged, diseased, and crossing branches (the "three Ds and one C"). To keep healthy trees and shrubs looking their best, your community garden group can learn basic, feet-on-the-ground minor pruning techniques. Hand pruners, pruning saws, loppers, and pole pruners are some of the common tools used for minor pruning.

quick tip

Cold frame designs can be downloaded at *www.woodworkersworkshop.com/resources/index.php?cat=388* and *www.greenfootsteps.com/cold-frame-design.html*.

Instructions for a do-it-yourself hoop house can be found here: *http://westsidegardener.com/howto/hoophouse.html*

Why prune?
- Safety: to remove low-hanging limbs, weak limbs that may fall, and those growing into power lines
- Appearance: to enhance tree shape (only advisable for young trees)
- Health: to remove dead, diseased, damaged, or crossing branches

When to prune
- Winter is a good time to check trees and locate problems
- Anytime there are dead, diseased, damaged, and crossing branches
- Late winter: before leaf buds open
- Fall to spring: when there are no leaves
- Midsummer: once new shoot growth becomes woody
- Do not prune a recently transplanted tree

Fertilizing

Never fertilize a newly planted tree. Wait at least one year for the tree to become established. Fertilizing will not solve problems caused by inadequate sunlight or water, air pollution, plant diseases, or insect attack. The young sapling, the mature healthy tree, and the declining tree each have different needs. Visible foliage symptoms will tell you if fertilizers are needed. Observe the leaf color; unusual yellowing, especially between the veins, may indicate a specific nutritional deficiency. Notice whether the old or new leaves are affected. Consult an arborist regarding a tree in trouble. A soil test from the tree pit will determine the fertilizers needed. ∎

iStockphoto.com

Newly planted trees require one inch of rain per week or equivalent supplemental watering during the first two years after planting. Be sure you have a plan in place to provide adequate water for new trees.

Go Gold

The PHS Gold Medal Plant Award program promotes trees, shrubs, and woody vines of outstanding merit. These plants are evaluated and chosen for superb eye-appeal, performance, and hardiness in the growing region of Zones 5 through 7, but many Gold Medal plants are hardy in a broader geographic range. Learn about these plants at *www.goldmedalplants.org*.

Chapter 5: Involving the Next Generation

Ideally your community garden will be around for years, even decades to come. To help make that happen, recruit the next generation of gardeners now. Once you tap into kid energy, you will find that young people feel strongly about improving their communities and creating beauty, and that younger children love digging in the dirt. Make their garden participation fun and give them plenty of positive reinforcement.

Before inviting children into the garden, make sure your bylaws state what role they will have in the garden. For instance, at what age is it permissible for a child to visit the garden unaccompanied? What types of activities are permitted?

If a good percentage of the community gardeners are parents, explore creating a children's plot. Having their own space enables kids to unleash their creativity and enthusiasm. Designate one or more adults to take on the role of plot supervisor.

Reach Out to Schools and Youth Groups

Many educators look for hands-on learning opportunities, and gardens present the perfect environment for teaching and learning a variety of subjects. Reach out to nearby schools and present your garden as a conveniently located option. In addition to the educational value of gardening, it may also satisfy district requirements that students complete a community service project. One suggestion for a service-learning project is using student help to research, plan, and implement garden cleanups or activities.

If schools are unable to fit you into their curriculum, you can pursue enriching their after-school program. Establishing a youth gardening group during this period has the advantage of not competing with a teacher's instructional time during the day. Consider enlisting student help to pick up litter at both their schoolyard and the garden, for example.

Giving schools and after-school programs plots of their own is wonderful because, unlike a schoolyard garden, you can recruit fellow community gardeners to tend it during the summer months. If everyone contributes just a little time, the garden will be ready for the new crop of kids in September.

Take advantage of the resources of organizations that already have extensive experience working with youth, such as Boy Scouts, Girl Scouts, and the 4-H. Reach out to these organizations to find out if there's interest in having their participants involved in your garden.

When you invite groups of children into the garden, consult with their teacher or chaperone about issuing permission slips for parents or guardians to sign. The slip should explain the general garden rules and expected conduct, and also state that the garden is not responsible for accidents, injuries, or mishaps that might occur.

If your garden isn't equipped for hands-on kid involvement, think creatively about other ways to include them. A guided tour can offer many lessons about biology, nutrition, and more. Art projects are another great way of connecting kids to the garden. They can paint a mural, put their handprints on decorative stones, or build birdfeeders. Finally, the garden is a tranquil setting perfect for reading and storytelling.

Don't limit your outreach to young children; teenagers are another group with much to learn from community gardening, as well as much to offer. They can take part in the same types of activities as the younger ones but geared to their age group. Helping them develop a sense of ownership of their project will go a long way toward getting them invested in the garden.

Tips for Incorporating Young People into the Garden

- Safety comes first. Teach them the proper way to handle tools, plants, etc.
- Stress to youngsters the importance of respecting people's labor and space.
- Break down instructions into small steps and provide a demonstration.
- Have children plant crops that grow quickly; that way they can observe the plant's life cycle. By snacking on the vegetables they've grown, children will better understand where food comes from and will appreciate the difference between fresh and store-bought food (you can even do a blind taste test with the kids).
- Use the garden to illustrate the connections between the plant and animal worlds, such as the role of beneficial insects and pollinators.
- Before starting a kids' garden, perform a soil test to check for lead and other heavy metals. Lead can be harmful, especially to toddlers and young children who put things into their mouths. Wash their hands often, particularly before meals, and rinse off toys that were in the soil.
- Kids can do a lot in the garden. In addition to planting and watering, involve them with mulching, raking, raised-bed building, and other tasks.

With a community garden, you have the opportunity to pass on a passion for gardening, an appreciation for nature, and lessons on the value of community.

See the Resources section for more on gardening with children.

Teens 4 Good: Growing Tomorrow's Leaders

A program of the Federation of Neighborhood Centers, Teens 4 Good was launched as a community garden in North Philadelphia and has evolved into a youth entrepreneurship and gardening venture that transforms urban vacant lots into gardens, farms, and multi-purpose green spaces. It engages young people in hands-on gardening, nutrition, and entrepreneurial activities.

The teens grow vegetables and herbs at garden sites and sell food to restaurants and farmers markets, as well as donate food to area food cupboards through the PHS City Harvest project. Teens 4 Good now operates at multiple sites in a number of city neighborhoods.

Teens 4 Good creates jobs for youth, increases access to nutritious food, and adds beauty to urban neighborhoods. It empowers young people to become leaders and to develop skills that enhance their communities.

Jamie McKnight, who coordinates the program, describes the effect it has on the teenagers: "The kids really enjoy working outdoors and learning how plants grow, and they also develop a good work ethic. They become more aware of their community and more interested in continuing their education."

For more information, visit *www.federationnc.org/Teens-4-Good.page*.

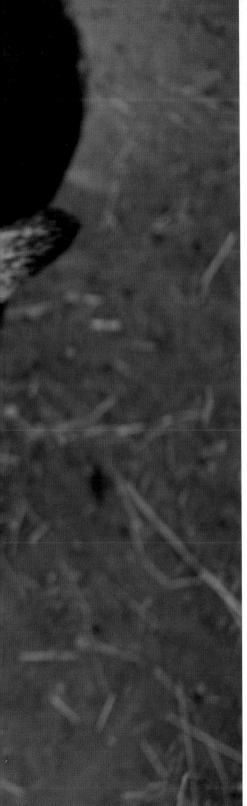

Two Goats Farm: Inviting the Neighbors In

When his daughter outgrew the playground at the edge of his property, Philadelphia resident Nick Rousch wanted to do something with the vacant space. At the time, the recession was hitting area residents hard, and Nick, who lives in the city's Germantown section, wanted to give neighbors a place to unwind and focus on something gratifying. A community garden fit the bill, and Nick set about establishing Two Goats Farm.

To get the garden off the ground, Nick enrolled in PHS's Garden Tenders program, where he attended classes and met like-minded community gardeners who helped him build raised beds on his lot. He also acquired additional land. Nick says that the enthusiasm of fellow gardeners and the community (as well as his own drive) provided the fuel that kept this major undertaking in motion.

Clearly, a sense of humor doesn't hurt either—Nick named the garden after his two goats, Tippy and Tulla. But the goats are more than just mascots, their manure provides a great garden fertilizer.

Now, two years after it began, Nick says the 15-plot garden "has become a place where people can come together to make the neighborhood a better place to live." Nick's generosity has turned an unused plot of land into a welcoming green haven for the whole community. ▮

Conclusion

Walking along a city street, few sights are as pleasing as a lush garden abundant with vegetables and flowers. Community gardeners throughout the world's cities have transformed neglected urban lots into oases that provide beauty and a place where city dwellers can come together. But it has become increasingly clear that gardens play vital roles beyond offering these aesthetic benefits.

The most frequently cited social benefit of community gardens is their power to create a strong connection among participants, who often come together across chasms of race, culture, and economic status to share the simple joys of gardening. This "social capital," though difficult to measure, is indeed an invaluable asset. These gardens build solidarity among their members and strengthen people's attachment, both to the garden itself and to each other. The collateral benefits of this sense of attachment extend to the neighborhood and city as a whole, as it encourages people to put down roots and invest in their communities.

Once the scene of rampant drug trafficking, the North Philadelphia neighborhood of Norris Square was a place few wanted to call home. It now boasts six prize-winning gardens created by residents on formerly unkempt, trash-strewn lots. The gardens have given people a place to come together and stake a claim on their community. "By working together we created something from nothing," says Iris Brown of Norris Square. "It's like an entirely different place now, and it all started with the gardens."

As discussed earlier, community gardens help support the larger urban economy by boosting property values, provide open space and improve the environment, promote health and safety, and offer educational opportunities for children and other populations. They are also an increasingly important part of the local food network, bridging the gap between farm and city.

To remain viable, these treasured spaces require investment and support. Municipalities can facilitate community gardening through simple, practical steps. They can revise cumbersome land-transfer systems that make it difficult to set aside land for gardens, make water accessible and affordable, and offer municipal compost and mulch. They can set aside space within parks for use as community gardens, just as they do for ball fields, tennis courts, and golf courses.

Community gardens enrich the landscapes of cities in so many ways, and not just for those lucky enough to have a plot. As Hou, Johnson, and Lawson write in *Greening Cities, Growing Communities* (2009), "A recurring feature in American cities, the community garden is not only a tangible resource for individuals and communities but also an organizing concept for new ideas about quality of life and urban sustainability." ∎

RESOURCES

About Community Gardens

Gröning, Gert. "Kleingärten." In *The Oxford Companion to the Garden*, p. 266. New York: Oxford University Press, USA, 2006.

Hester, Randolph T. *Design for Ecological Democracy.* Boston: Massachusetts Institute of Technology, 2006.

Hou, Jeffrey, Julie M. Johnson, and Laura J. Lawson. *Greening Cities, Growing Communities: Learning from Seattle's Urban Community Gardens.* Seattle and London: University of Washington Press, 2009.

Hynes, H. Patricia. *A Patch of Eden: America's Inner City Gardeners.* White River Junction, VT: Chelsea Green Pub, 1996.

Lawson, Laura J. *City Bountiful: A Century of Community Gardening in America.* Berkeley: University of California Press, 2005.

Taylor, Patrick. "Allotment." In *The Oxford Companion to the Garden*, p. 7–8. New York: Oxford University Press, 2006.

Tucker, David M. "Garden and Community." In *Kitchen Gardening in America: A History, 155–165.* Ames: Iowa State University Press, 1993.

Warner, Sam Bass. *To Dwell Is to Garden: A History of Boston's Community Gardens.* Boston: Northeastern University Press, 1987.

Weissman, Evan. "Community Gardens." In *Encyclopedia of Organic, Sustainable, and Local Food*, 189–193. Santa Barbara, CA: Greenwood, 2010.

Composting

Appelhof, Mary. *Worms Eat My Garbage.* 2nd ed. Kalamazoo, MI: Flower Press, 1997.

Composting 101. "The Dirt on Composting." A complete home composting guide, this site offers practical information for converting yard, garden and kitchen waste into soil-building compost. *www.composting101.com/*

U.S. Environmental Protection Agency. "Wastes - Resource Conservation - Reduce, Reuse, Recycle - Composting." Website contains information on home composting, relevant law, and environmental benefits. *www.epa.gov/epawaste/conserve/rrr/composting/index.htm*

Cover Crops

Sullivan, Preston. "Overview of Cover Crops and Green Manures." 2003. National Sustainable Agriculture Information Service. This publication is a summary of the principal uses and benefits of cover crops and green manures. Includes print and web resources for more information. *http://attra.ncat.org/attra-pub/covercrop.html*

Edible Landscaping

Beck, Travis, and Martin F. Quigley. "Edible Landscaping, HYG-1255-02." Ohio State University Extension Factsheet. Ohio State University Extension. Edible landscaping offers an alternative to conventional residential landscapes that are designed solely for ornamental purposes. *http://ohioline.osu.edu/hyg-fact/1000/1255.html*

Creasy, Rosalind. *The Complete Book of Edible Landscaping.* San Francisco: Sierra Club Books, 1982.

———. "Edible Landscaping for the Home Gardener." Edible landscaping tips, food, and gardening advice from Rosalind Creasy, a pioneer in the field of edible landscaping. *www.rosalindcreasy.com/*

Hemenway, Toby. *Gaia's Garden: A Guide to Home-Scale Permaculture. Second Edition,* White River Junction, VT: Chelsea Green Publishing Co., 2009.

National Gardening Association. "Edible Landscaping with Charlie Nardozzi." Articles, questions and answers, and resource guide on edible landscapes and vegetable gardening. *www.garden.org/ediblelandscaping/*

Flowers and Mixed-Use Gardens

Brooklyn Botanic Garden. *Gourmet Herbs: Classic and Unusual Herbs for Your Garden and Your Table.* Brooklyn Botanic Garden publications handbook #167. Brooklyn, NY: Brooklyn Botanic Garden, 2001.

Damrosch, Barbara. *The Garden Primer: The Completely Revised Gardener's Bible.* New York: Workman Publishing Company, 2008.

Evergreen (Association). "Community Gardens: Themes & Ideas, 2001." From Toronto, Canada, Evergreen is a nonprofit environmental organization focusing on bringing nature to urban environments. Website includes ideas for vegetable and herb gardens; wildlife habitat gardens; container gardens; seniors' gardens; children's gardens; rooftop gardens. *www.evergreen.ca/docs/res/CG6-Community-Gardening-Ideas.pdf*

Hill, Lewis. *The Flower Gardener's Bible: Time-Tested Techniques, Creative Designs, and Perfect Plants for Colorful Gardens.* North Adams, MA: Storey Books, 2003.

Food Security

Astyk, Sharon. *A Nation of Farmers: Defeating the Food Crisis on American Soil.* Gabriola Island, BC: New Society Publishers, 2009.

"Community Food Security Coalition," The Community Food Security Coalition is a North American coalition of diverse people and organizations working from the local to international levels to build community food security. *www.foodsecurity.org*

"Growing Power." Growing Power is a national nonprofit organization and land trust supporting people and the environments in which they live by helping to provide equal access to healthy, high-quality, safe and affordable food for people in all communities. *www.growingpower.org*

Solomon, Steve. *Gardening When It Counts: Growing Food in Hard Times.* Gabriola Island, BC: New Society Publishers, 2005.

Hallberg, Basil. "Using Community Gardens to Augment Food Security Efforts in Low-Income Communities." Masters of Urban and Regional Planning Major Paper, Virginia Tech, 2009. This paper explores the potential of community gardening as a tool to augment food security efforts within low-income communities. *www.ipg.vt.edu/Papers/Hallberg%20Major%20Paper.pdf*

Kimbrell, Andrew, ed. *Fatal Harvest. The Tragedy of Industrial Agriculture.* Sausalito, CA: Foundation for Deep Ecology, 2002.

General Gardening Information

Bradley, Fern Marshall. *Rodale's Vegetable Garden Problem Solver: The Best and Latest Advice for Beating Pests, Diseases, and Weeds and Staying a Step Ahead of Trouble in the Garden.* New York, NY: Rodale, 2007.

Coleman, Eliot. *The Winter Harvest Handbook: Year-Round Vegetable Production Using Deep-Organic Techniques and Unheated Greenhouses.* White River Junction, VT: Chelsea Green Pub, 2009.

"Cooperative Extension System Offices." Use this U.S. Department of Agriculture site to locate your nearest Cooperative Extension office. County extension offices are excellent sources of information on gardening in your area. *www.csrees. usda.gov/Extension/index.html*

Garden Guides. "Starting Seeds Indoors." Useful instructions for getting your garden started by propagating seeds indoors. *www.gardenguides.com/3021-starting-seeds-indoors.html*

Guerra, Michael. *Edible Container Garden: Growing Fresh Food in Small Spaces.* New York: Simon & Schuster, 2000.

Lanza, Patricia. *Lasagna Gardening for Small Spaces: A Layering System for Big Results in Small Gardens and Containers.* Emmaus, PA: Rodale, 2002.

Lloyd, Christopher. *Succession Planting: For Year-Round Pleasure.* Portland, OR: Timber Press, 2005.

MacCubbin, Tom. "Grow Your Own Oriental Vegetables." Orient Magazine, Asian vegetable tips. *www.orientmag.com/food1.asp*

"National Arboretum – USDA Plant Hardiness Zone Map." U.S. National Arboretum. This Hardiness Zone Map is an essential resource for gardeners. It indicates the cold hardiness ratings (zones) for selected woody plants. Click on the map of the United States Plant Hardiness Zones, or search by your state, to learn the hardiness zone for your garden. *www.usna.usda.gov/Hardzone/ushzmap.html*

Oehler, Mike. 2007. *The Earth-Sheltered Solar Greenhouse Book: How to Build an Energy-Free Year-Round Greenhouse.* Bonners Ferry, ID: Mole Pub. Co.

Pennsylvania State University, College of Agricultural Sciences. "Garden Use of Treated Lumber." Addresses commonly asked questions on treated lumber for use in gardens. *http://cropsoil.psu.edu/extension/facts/treated-lumber .pdf/view?searchterm=treated%20lumber*

Pepper, Jane G. *Jane Pepper's Garden: Getting the Most Pleasure and Growing Results from Your Garden Every Month of the Year.* Philadelphia: Camino Books, 1997.

Rosen, Carl J. "Lead in the Home Garden and Urban Soil Environment." Factsheet. University of Minnesota Extension Service. Twin Cities Campus: University of Minnesota, Revised 2002. *www.extension.umn.edu/distribution/horticul ture/DG2543.html*

Salt, Bernard. *Gardening Under Plastic: How to Use Fleece, Films, Clothes [i.e. Cloches] and Polytunnels.* London: Batsford, 1999.

Saling, Travis. "How to Build a PVC Hoophouse for Your Garden." The Westside Gardener. Simple instructions for building a PVC hoophouse to extend your growing season. *http://westsidegardener.com/howto/hoophouse.html*

Schrock, Denny. "Building and Using Hotbeds and Cold Frames." University of Missouri, Extension Service. Factsheet on extending the growing season by using hotbeds and coldframes. *http://extension.missouri.edu/publications/DisplayPub .aspx?P=g6965*

Stell, Elizabeth. *Secrets to Great Soil: A Grower's Guide to Composting, Mulching, and Creating Healthy, Fertile Soil for Your Garden and Lawn.* Storey's gardening skills illustrated. Pownal, VT: Storey Pub, 1998.

Toronto FoodShare. "Ten Tools Every Community Gardener & Garden Needs." American Community Gardening Association. *http://communitygarden.org/docs/10tools.pdf*

Turner, Carole B. *Seed Sowing and Saving: Step-by-Step Techniques for Collecting and Growing More Than 100 Vegetables, Flowers, and Herbs.* Storey's gardening skills illustrated. Pownal, VT: Storey Communications, 1998.

Vegetable Gardening Guru. "Planning a Vegetable Garden." Includes suggestions for creating a garden plan. *www.vegetablegardeningguru.com/getting-started.html*

Group Development and Finding Support

Abi-Nader, Jeanette, and American Community Gardening Association. *Growing Communities Curriculum: Community Building and Organizational Development Through Community Gardening.* Philadelphia, PA: American Community Gardening Association, 2001.

American Community Gardening Association. "Starting a Community Garden." Designed to give many different groups the basic information they need to get their gardening project off the ground. *www.communitygarden.org/learn/starting-a-community-garden.php*

"Clinton Community Garden." See this community garden website for its garden rules and bylaws. *http://clintoncommunitygarden.org*

"Gardening Matters," Minneapolis-based organization offers online library of resources, including public policies supporting community gardens. *www.gardeningmatters.org/*

Keep America Beautiful. "Toolbox for Community Change, Community Gardens." Practical advice, great ideas, and time-tested tools for creating community gardens. *www.kab.org/site/PageServer?pagename=TB_Community_Gardens*

Krome, Margaret, Teresa Maurer, and Katie Wied. "Building Sustainable Farms, Ranches and Communities: Federal Programs for Sustainable Agriculture, Forestry, Entrepreneurship, Conservation and Community Development," U.S. Department of Agriculture, Sustainable Agriculture Research and Education program (SARE). 2009. *www.sare.org/publications/ruralplaces.htm*

Lakey, Berit. "Meeting Facilitation: The No-Magic Method," Training for Change, n.d. *www.trainingforchange.org/meeting_facilitation*

McKelvey, Bill. "Community Gardening Toolkit." University of Missouri Extension Service. Comprehensive information source for starting and maintaining community gardens. *http://extension.missouri.edu/publications/DisplayPub.aspx?P=MP906*

"Neighborhood Gardens Association/A Philadelphia Land Trust." The Neighborhood Gardens Association (NGA) is a nonprofit corporation whose mission is the continuity and long-term preservation of community-managed gardens and green spaces in Philadelphia neighborhoods. *www.ngalandtrust.org*

"New York Restoration Project." NYRP restores, revitalizes and develops under-resourced parks and community gardens throughout the city's five boroughs, working to ensure that every New York City resident, family and neighborhood has access to vibrant, green spaces. *www.nyrp.org.*

Payne, Karen, and American Community Gardening Association. *Cultivating Community: Principles and Practices for Community Gardening as a Community-Building Tool.* Philadelphia, PA: American Community Gardening Association, 2001.

"P-Patch Trust." P-Patch Trust works to acquire, build, preserve and protect community gardens in Seattle's neighborhoods. *www.ppatchtrust.org*

Seattle Department of Neighborhoods. "P-Patch Community Gardens." The P-Patch Community Gardening Program, in conjunction with P-Patch Trust, a nonprofit organization, oversees 73 P-Patches distributed throughout the city, equaling approximately 23 acres and serving 2,056 households. *www.seattle.gov/neighborhoods/ppatch/*

Surls, Rachel. "Community Garden Start-Up Guide." University of California Cooperative Extension Service. This community gardening guide is intended to help neighborhood groups and organizations along the path to starting and sustaining a community garden. It includes a sample community gardening contract for participants. *http://celosangeles.ucdavis.edu/garden/articles/startup_guide.html*

Urban Land Institute. *Ten Principles for Successful Public/Private Partnerships.* Washington, DC: Urban Land Institute, 2005.

Walljasper, Jay, and Project for Public Spaces. *The Great Neighborhood Book: A Do-It-Yourself Guide to Placemaking.* Gabriola Island, BC: New Society Publishers, 2007.

Habitat Gardens

"Build a Bat House." Befriend the bat, a natural pest controller; a single brown bat can eat up to 1,000 mosquitoes in one hour. Website gives instructions on building bat houses. *www.eparks.org/wildlife_protection/wildlife_facts/bats/bat_house.asp*

Druse, Kenneth. *The Natural Habitat Garden.* 1st ed. New York: Clarkson Potter, 1994.

Duerksen, Christopher J. *Nature-Friendly Communities: Habitat Protection and Land Use.* Washington, DC: Island Press, 2005.

Ellis, Barbara W. *Attracting Birds and Butterflies: How to Plan and Plant a Backyard Habitat.* Taylor's weekend gardening guides. Boston, MA: Houghton Mifflin Co, 1997.

Jacobsen, Rowan. *Fruitless Fall: The Collapse of the Honey Bee and the Coming Agricultural Crisis.* 1st ed. New York: Bloomsbury, 2008.

National Wildlife Federation. "Create a Certified Wildlife Habitat," Whether you have an apartment balcony or a 20-acre farm, you can create a garden that attracts wildlife and helps restore habitat in commercial and residential areas. *www.nwf.org/Get-Outside/Outdoor-Activities/Garden-for-Wildlife/Create-a-Habitat.aspx*

"Urban Bee Gardens." This site is a practical guide to introducing bees to your garden. It also has information on bee garden research. *http://nature.berkeley.edu/urbanbeegardens/*

Health Benefits

Prevention Institute. The Built Environment and Health: 11 Profiles of Neighborhood Transformation, July 2004. Highlights neighborhood-level changes to the built environment that can have a positive influence on the health of community residents, especially in low-income communities. The case study "Gardens for Growing Healthy Communities" profiles the transformation of vacant lots into community gardens in Denver, CO. *www.preventioninstitute.org/component/jlibrary/article/id-114/127.html*

Rice, Jay Stone, Linda L. Remy, and Lisa Ann Whittlesey. "Substance Abuse, Offender Rehabilitation, and Horticultural Therapy Practice." In *Horticulture as Therapy: Principles And Practice,* 257–284. New York: Food Products Press, 1998.

Rain Gardens

Dunnett, Nigel. *Rain Gardens: Managing Water Sustainably in the Garden and Designed Landscape.* Portland, OR: Timber Press, 2007.

"Rain Garden Network." What is a rain garden and why should we plant one? Site is a resource for stormwater solutions individuals and groups can install. *www.raingardennetwork.com*

Wallace, Terry. *The Rain Garden Planner: Seven Steps to Conserving and Managing Water in the Garden.* Atglen, PA: Schiffer Pub, 2009.

School Gardens

Bucklin-Sporer, Arden. *How to Grow a School Garden: A Complete Guide for Parents and Teachers.* Portland, OR: Timber Press, 2010.

Johnson, Katherine A. *The Chicago School Garden Initiative: A Collaborative Model for Developing School Gardens That Work.* Glencoe, IL: Chicago Botanic Garden, 2003.

Kiefer, Joseph, and American Community Gardening Association. *Digging Deeper: Integrating Youth Gardens into Schools & Communities, a Comprehensive Guide.* Montpelier, VT: Food Works; Common Roots Press, 1998.

Martin Luther King, Jr. Middle School, Berkeley, California. "Edible Schoolyard." The Edible Schoolyard is a one-acre organic garden and kitchen classroom for urban public school students at Martin Luther King, Jr. Middle School in Berkeley, CA. *www.edibleschoolyard.org*

Metallo, Mike. "Cultivating Success in a School Garden." National Gardening Association. A well-designed school garden program, closely aligned with learning goals, is a valuable tool to help young people turn book knowledge into experiential knowledge. *www.kidsgardening.com/Dig/digdetail.taf?Type=Art&id=2294*

Soil Testing

McGrath, Mike. "Be Smart! Be Thrifty! Be Really Cool! Get Your Soil Tested!" You Bet Your Garden, WHYY. Lists state soil test information for the Mid-Atlantic. Contact your local county extension service for details. *www.whyy.org/91FM/ybyg/soiltests2.html*

Pennsylvania State University, College of Agricultural Sciences. "Agricultural Analytical Services Lab." The Agricultural Analytical Services Lab at Penn State offers a standard soil test. *www.aasl.psu.edu/SSFT.HTM*

Rosen, Carl J. "Lead in the Home Garden and Urban Soil Environment." University of Minnesota Extension. 2010. *www.extension.umn.edu/distribution/horticulture/DG2543.html*

"University of Massachusetts Extension Service, Soil and Plant Tissue Testing Laboratory." Testing service and price list; includes testing for lead in soil. *www.umass.edu/soiltest/list_of_services.htm*

Strengthening Community

"Homeless Garden Project." Recognized as a model program by World Hunger Year, this Santa Cruz, California-based organization practices and teaches economic and environmental sustainability and provides homeless men and women with job training and transitional employment. *http://homelessgardenproject.org*

Klindienst, Patricia. *The Earth Knows My Name: Food, Culture, and Sustainability in the Gardens of Ethnic Americans.* Boston: Beacon Press, 2006.

Lyson, Thomas A. *Civic Agriculture: Reconnecting Farm, Food, and Community.* Medford, MA: Tufts University Press, 2004.

Malakoff, David. "What Good Is Community Greening?" *Community Greening Review* 13 (2004): 16–20.

Pennsylvania Horticultural Society. "Community Gardens of the 21st Century: Growing for the Future." Strategy for a Green City. Philadelphia: Pennsylvania Horticultural Society, 2008. *www.pennsylvaniahorticulturalsociety.org/phlgreen/Community21stCent.pdf*

Trees and Shrubs

Brand, Mark H. "UConn Plant Database of Trees, Shrubs and Vines." University of Connecticut. This site provides information on the ornamental attributes, appropriate use, and identification of landscape plants. *www.hort.uconn.edu/plants/index.html*

Dirr, Michael A. *Dirr's Hardy Trees and Shrubs: An Illustrated Encyclopedia*. Portland, OR: Timber Press, 1997.

-----. *Manual of Woody Landscape Plants: Their Identification, Ornamental Characteristics, Culture, Propagation and Uses*. 6th Edition. Champagne, IL: Stipes Publishing, 2009.

National Gardening Association. "NGA Plant Finder," Search tool for plants, including trees and shrubs. *www.garden.org/plantfinder/*

Pennsylvania Horticultural Society. Gold Medal Plant Award program includes searchable database of trees, shrubs, and vines. Website includes tree-planting videos and tree-care information. Tree Tenders® training program educates volunteers to care for trees. *www.PHSonline.org*

Trees are Good. "Tree Care Information." Educational website of the International Society of Arboriculture. *http://treesaregood.com/treecare/tree_selection.aspx*

Urban, James. *Up by Roots: Healthy Soils and Trees in the Built Environment*. Champaign, IL: International Society of Arboriculture, 2008.

Urban Food Production and Sustainability

Barlett, Peggy F. *Urban Place: Reconnecting with the Natural World*. Cambridge, MA: MIT Press, 2005.

Feenstra, Gail Whiting. *Entrepreneurial Community Gardens: Growing Food, Skills, Jobs and Communities*. Oakland, CA: University of California, Division of Agriculture and Natural Resources, 1999.

Flores, H. C. *Food Not Lawns: How to Turn Your Yard into a Garden and Your Neighborhood into a Community*. White River Junction, VT: Chelsea Green Pub. Company, 2006.

Forsyth, Phil. "PHIGBLOG; edible landscapes, urban farms, food growing in Philadelphia." PHIGBLOG is about growing food in Philadelphia; the blog is a news service covering urban farming, edible landscaping, and related themes, as well as a guidebook for city folks to learn more about how to grow their own food. *http://phigblog.com*

Henderson, Elizabeth. *Sharing the Harvest: A Guide to Community Supported Agriculture*. White River Junction, VT: Chelsea Green, 1999.

National Gardening Association. *The Impact of Home and Community Gardening in America*. South Burlington, VT: National Gardening Association, 2009. Report looks at food gardener demographics, reasons for gardening, where and how Americans garden. One million households garden in a community garden plot. *www.gardenresearch.com/files/2009-Impact-of-Gardening-in-America-White-Paper.pdf*

"Philadelphia Orchard Project." The Philadelphia Orchard Project plants orchards in the city of Philadelphia that grow healthy food, green spaces and community food security. *www.phillyorchards.org*

Sustainable Sites Initiative. "The Case for Sustainable Landscapes." 2009. The Sustainable Sites Initiative (SITES) has developed criteria for sustainable land practices that will enable built landscapes to support natural ecological functions. This document provides a set of arguments—economic, environmental, and social—for the adoption of sustainable land practices. *www.sustainablesites.org/report*

-----. "The Sustainable Sites Initiative: Guidelines and Performance Benchmarks 2009." Includes a rating system for credits which the SITES Pilot Program (through June 2012) will test for refinement before a formal release to the market place. *www.sustainablesites.org/report*

Youth Engagement

Benjamin, Joan. "Sustainable Agriculture Resources and Programs for K-12 Youth," U.S. Department of Agriculture, Sustainable Agriculture Research and Education program (SARE). 2009.
http://www.sare.org/publications/edguide.htm

Campbell, Lindsay K. "Youth Empowerment Through Urban Agriculture: Red Hook Community Farm." In *Restorative Commons: Creating Health and Well-being Through Urban Landscapes*, 202–215. Newtown Square, PA: USDA Forest Service, 2009.

Cornell University. "Garden Mosaics: Garden Science, Intergenerational Learning, Action Learning, Multicultural Education." Connects youth and elders to investigate the mosaic of plants, people, and cultures in gardens. *www.gardenmosaics.cornell.edu*

"EcoExpress." The core of EcoExpress lies in real world stories about people who are taking on environmental challenges by getting involved. Engaging, inspiring, and anchored in Pennsylvania's environment and ecology standards to bring classroom subjects to life. *www.ecoexpress.org*

Gale, Greg, and the Food Project. *Growing Together: A Guide for Building Inspired, Diverse, and Productive Youth Communities*. Lincoln, MA: The Food Project, 2000.

Junior Master Gardener. "JMGkids Online." Junior Master Gardener curricula include: independent and group learning experiences; life/skill and career exploration; service learning opportunities for youth; correlation to state teaching standards. *www.jmgkids.us*

Louv, Richard. *Last Child in the Woods: Saving Our Children from Nature-Deficit Disorder*. 1st ed. Chapel Hill, NC: Algonquin Books of Chapel Hill, 2005.

National Gardening Association. "Research Supporting the Benefits of School Gardens." Kidsgardening.org. *www.kidsgardening.com/Dig/digdetail.taf?Type=Art&id=2293*

Pennsylvania Horticultural Society. "Youth in the Garden: Cultivating the Environmental Stewards of Tomorrow." Strategy for a Green City. Pennsylvania Horticultural Society, 2008. *www.pennsylvaniahorticulturalsociety.org/phlgreen/youthinthegarden.pdf*

TLC Family. "Nature Crafts." Use nature's bounty to create spore prints, apple tree centerpieces, and more. *http://tlc.howstuffworks.com/family/nature-crafts.htm*

Index